Twayne's English Authors Series

EDITOR OF THIS VOLUME

Kinley E. Roby

Northeastern University

Rebecca West

TEAS 296

Rebecca West

PR 6045 .E8 Z63
Deakin, Motley F.
Rebecca West /

REBECCA WEST

By MOTLEY F. DEAKIN

University of Florida

RITTER LIBRARY
BALDWIN-WALLACE COLLEGE

TWAYNE PUBLISHERS

A DIVISION OF G. K. HALL & CO., BOSTON

Copyright © 1980 by G. K. Hall & Co.

Published in 1980 by Twayne Publishers,
A Division of G. K. Hall & Co.
All Rights Reserved

Printed on permanent/durable acid-free paper and bound
in the United States of America

First Printing

Library of Congress Cataloging in Publication Data

Deakin, Motley F
Rebecca West.

(Twayne's English authors series ; TEAS 296)
Bibliography: p. 178-80
Includes index.
1. West, Rebecca, pseud.—Criticism and
interpretation.
PR6045.E8Z63   828'.91209   79-27601
ISBN 0-8057-6788-6

Contents

About the Author

Motley Deakin is a member of the English Department at the University of Florida. A graduate of Snow College and Brigham Young University, he received his M.A. and Ph.D. from the University of California at Berkeley. He participated in the University of Maryland Foreign Study Center in Paris, France, and served as a Civilian Education Advisor in Heidelberg, Germany. He has taught at the College of the Holy Names, the University of Texas at El Paso, and the University of Florida.

Professor Deakin has published articles on Henry James, prepared the Introduction for *The Home Book of the Picturesque* published in the Scholarly Facsimile and Reprint series, and coedited with Peter Lisca a collection of essays in honor of Harry Warfel entitled *From Irving to Steinbeck*. He is a member of the Modern Language Association and various other professional organizations.

Preface

For all her fame and official recognition as a writer, Dame Rebecca West has received little attention from the critics. There are reasons. Her interests are so varied that anyone wishing to examine her work in toto must adopt some of her encyclopedic interest as she moves from literary criticism to the theory that informs it, from history to biography and fiction. He must be willing to follow her as she develops her responses to areas of knowledge as different as aesthetics, psychology, and sociology. Just as her interests are diverse, so also are the places in which one finds her publications. In spite of the fact that she has published over twenty books, at least half of her work still lies uncollected in scores of newspapers and journals in both Britain and the United States. And although she has long since gained acceptance in the literary circles of London and New York, she still most often is identified by that lesser term *journalist,* suggesting that much of her work is ephemeral in nature and thus not justifying serious critical attention.

Despite these difficulties, one who is willing to seek out her myriad efforts will find ideas, opinions, and perceptions articulated in a lucid, vigorous, sometimes intemperate, often exciting prose. The reader may not always agree with her, but he still will be challenged and at times enlightened. He will find her most rewarding, I think, for her analysis of twentieth-century European history, particularly for those phases of it—the rise of modern technological society and the counterefforts it stimulated to mitigate its dehumanizing influences, the wave of totalitarianism that surged over central and eastern Europe, the corrosion of treason with its threat to basic human loyalties— which interested her most. Endemic in her view of history is a dark strain of pessimism with its roots in her view of humanity, its nature and conditions.

To balance this pessimism, the reader can look to her support of the feminist movement, for to her the feminist principle is a positive force promoting life. This support is constant, though its intensity waxed and waned as her interests and personal situation changed. However this may be, she does have a significant place in the history of the feminist movement which must be noted and respected, even though certain contemporary feminist interests must be anathema to her. As a woman, her impulse is not to separate and discriminate. Instead, she desires to participate in what she may recognize as a dualistic world, but which is also a world of individuals, each capable of a uniqueness and independence that for her is vital to both her personal life and her writing.

In her expression of a world in flux, at once decaying and growing, anxious to throw off Victorian restrictions yet not too sure what it would do with the freedom it had gained or what it could create to replace what it was in such a hurry to abandon, Rebecca West is typical of her generation. But of one thing she was certain; she would make of her life and her talent the most she could. She would not be held back by tradition or restrictive social views. In this determination she was like many other women of her generation who wanted to be free to seize opportunities denied to their mothers. Her choice of profession was not so radical. Women had won already a respected position in the world of letters. Still, to choose journalism, that branch of letters of less repute, and then engage in political polemics, as she did, was to risk social respectability. She took the risk and survived to be addressed one day as Dame Rebecca West.

She was one among a remarkable group of women in her generation. Lady Astor, for example, broke the political barriers that until then had kept Parliament a men's club. Other women of high rank began soiling their hands in business; they did everything from setting up Bible shops to owning creameries and jam factories, admittedly a gentle break with the past. Those of lesser rank flocked into the offices to operate the new machines, the telephone and the typewriter, and to take charge of the filing systems. A few found their way into the professions.

Those women with literary ambitions could publish journals as Dora Marsden did, or, like Lady Nancy Cunard, set up a press and publish books in what must have been a quieter moment of what her contemporaries considered to be a scandalous life. More proper ladies like Lady Cynthia Asquith wrote, when asked, their children's books and their biographies of the royal family. Women closer to West's interests and abilities are Winifred Holtby, Vera Brittain, and Storm Jameson. They all wrote fiction and they all were associated with journalism or publishing houses. They made their way, more or less diffident about their abilities, more or less conscious of the liabilities they faced as women. Virginia Woolf is of a different order; West admired and praised her. Katherine Mansfield is more similar — a writer of fiction, a reviewer of books—particularly in her liberated personal life. Rose Macaualy also bears comparison. Her interests are as various as those of Rebecca West. She has a similar intellectual alertness and satiric bent, but seems more witty and more apt to put a distance between herself and general topical interests.

With her contemporaries Rebecca West held her own. She sensed more of a challenge in the generation preceding, a challenge and also a debt. Of that generation, those writers to whom she seemed to feel most affinity were all men: Arnold Bennett, George Bernard Shaw, and most intensely H. G. Wells. These three, plus John Galsworthy, are her "uncles," her surrogate literary fathers. With them she felt she had to come to terms. Their critical examination of their world, the world she had inherited, and their attempts to reform it, was the social stance she at first accepted and tried to adapt to her own feminist purposes. But gradually she abandoned that stance, perhaps because she lacked her "uncles'" optimism about human nature, and moved back to a more conservative position from which she could still launch her critical barbs but need not advocate an alternative to what she deplored. As she had experienced it, change, however well intentioned, however well thought out, too often precipitated disaster.

My study of her work is structured on two assumptions. Her writing can be divided into chronological periods, each of which is dominated by one of her major interests: feminism, literary criticism, history, treason. Her writing on each of these interests I have examined in chronological order. One dominant interest, fiction, does not fit this chronological pattern. Instead, it remains an activity constant throughout her life, occupying a unique relationship to her other work. Typically she would examine and report on her current interest, then attempt to generalize and judge, and finally to reembody this interest in the imaginative form of fiction. Her fiction is characteristically a personalized distillation of her journalistic interests, often reflecting personal experience as well. Therefore, I have separated her fiction from her other work and have examined it in the last part of this study.

MOTLEY F. DEAKIN

University of Florida

Chronology

CHAPTER 1

Feminist

I *Public Career*

REBECCA West appeared on Britain's literary scene at what for her and the feminist movement was a propitious moment. Only nineteen years old, already an ardent advocate of women's suffrage, she began her career in letters just when the cry "Votes for Women" was echoing most shrilly across Britain. Nor was her entrance hesitant; from its inception her advocacy had an authority and assurance, a directness of purpose—an acerbity, even—hardly to be expected from one so young and of her embattled sex. Yet what better apprenticeship could she, now famous for her skill in incisive argument and sharp retort, have served than as an advocate of a cause as controversial and as likely to exact strong commitment as women's suffrage? Where better could she have honed her convictions and her talent to as fine an edge?

II *Early Life*

She was born Cicily Isabel Fairfield on December 21, 1892, in London, England. Her parents were talented and of good family. Her father, Charles, was of an old Anglo-Irish family that could trace its origins on the paternal side back to Slavic Wends or Serbs. He had served as an army officer in Britain and abroad, including a period as observer with the Confederate forces in the American Civil War. He was a scholar and writer. Though his daughter has attested to his intellectual brilliance, he proved temperamentally incapable of providing his wife and children with financial security, failing as he did to hold any position for long and yielding to an urge to speculate in unfortunate economic ventures. Her mother, Isabella, was of good Scottish family. She had great strength of character and gave the family what stability it had. An accomplished musician, she was a pianist of what her daughter thought to be professional quality. Cicily was the youngest of three sisters. One of her sisters became a teacher, the other a doctor. Cicily Fairfield's earliest memories were of living in London, memories that, as she said later, were darkened by the tragedies of her parents. Her father's life gradually disintegrated and he died alone in Liverpool. Her mother returned to her native city Edinburgh to face illness and poverty.

Suffering from tuberculosis, Cicily was in and out of school, ending her education at George Watson's Ladies College, after which she went to London to study acting at the Royal Academy of Dramatic Arts. She was on the stage for only a short time, though it was long enough to play the role of Rebecca West in Ibsen's *Rosmersholm,* a character whose name she soon took as her own. Leaving the theater, she joined the staff of the feminist periodical the *Freewoman* late in 1911. She used the name Rebecca West to conceal her new activities from her mother as well as to avoid what she thought was the excessive niceness of her real name, Cicily Fairfield. Her mother would not have objected to her being a writer, for as West said years later, "I write because all my family do, it is in the blood,"[1] but she would have objected to her daughter's association with a militantly feminist publication like the *Freewoman.*

III   *Early Feminist Writing*

Cicily Fairfield's first review signed "Rebecca West" appeared in February 1912. Like her other early reviews, it combines advocacy of the Suffragist cause with literary criticism. These reviews in the *Freewoman* range from an attack on Harold Owen's antifeminist *Woman Adrift* to an evaluation of Ezra Pound's translation of Guido Cavalcanti's poetry. This new voice in the *Freewoman* quickly caught the attention of a few influential, discriminating readers, including H. G. Wells, but the audience for the *Freewoman* was limited and it soon ceased publication.

In September 1912 Rebecca West moved to the *Clarion,* a Socialist weekly, where she could write about topical events as well as review books. In the *Clarion* she made a fortunate choice.

Founded by the popular journalist Robert Blatchford, the newspaper was a well-known and respected weekly with an average sale of 30,000 copies. West's essays appeared in each edition between September 1912 and December 1913. To read these thirty-four essays consecutively is to experience a vivid, exciting, sometimes shrill statement on feminism. In part it is a vivid description of what happened in these exciting months as seen by one who was certainly partial, but was perceptive as well; in part it is a strongly argued advocacy of the Suffragist's cause. She was not an activist in the sense that so many of the other Suffragettes were; she did not chain herself to iron fences or throw stones through shop windows or march to confrontations. Instead, she observed, she assessed, she argued, she attacked with her pen. These essays are perhaps not the best statement of her feminist convictions that she has made, but they do constitute her most sustained statement on the subject.

In the essays on feminism Rebecca West has written since then, the temper of her statements has mellowed and the authorial stance she assumes has shifted from that of an advocate doing battle for a worthy cause to that of an authority responding to solicitation. In the early 1920s she had planned to assemble her ideas on feminism in a work she would entitle *Second Thoughts on Feminism,* but she never completed the project. Thus her writings on this topic are still scattered through a large number of periodicals and journals. As a result, many of them are not well known today. But they were read in their time and they established her reputation as a feminist, a reputation significant enough to win the following dedication from George E. G. Catlin for his edition of Mary Wollstonecraft's *The Rights of Women* and John Stuart Mill's *The Subjection of Women:* "To Rebecca West who stands, in this generation, for that tradition which Mary Wollstonecraft and Mill have handed down."[2]

IV *British Suffragist Movement*

The tradition Mr. Catlin refers to is long and filled with distinguished names. The subjection of women against which Mary Wollstonecraft and her successors fought had its sources in a variety of attitudes and circumstances fostered by men: woman was the bearer of children, the maker of the home, the weaker sex, the object of love and the source of pleasure, the citadel of moral virtue, the temptress, the adored one. With the increase of wealth and leisure in the eighteenth century the fortunate woman accepted increasingly the role of the idle, elegant lady, but the source of this growing wealth and leisure, commerce and industry, pushed hordes of milady's less fortunate sisters into the factories and the shops. Legally women were disenfranchised, not equal to men before the law. A wife was forced to give her husband complete control of her own wealth, including the wedding ring she wore on her finger, and was not permitted even to maintain legal custody of her own body. Her husband could divorce her for infidelity, but however much of a libertine he may have been, she had no legal recourse. The Church, the law, custom, economics, man's egotism: all conspired to keep her in subjection.

The revolutions at the end of the eighteenth century created the opening wedge in woman's fight for equality. That men had fought for and won some measure of equal rights and equal freedom encouraged women to seek the same. Mary Wollstonecraft, a daughter of those revolutions, gave women their first effective argument: reason, unchanged and eternal, is not of a sexual nature, and therefore women, as well as men, are rational beings. Sharing with men the immortality of their souls, women had the duty to cultivate, through reason, the perfectibility of those souls. Her American counterpart, Margaret Fuller, put the argument in terms even more appropriate to the nineteenth century: "What Woman needs is not as a woman to act or rule, but as a nature to grow, as an intellect to discern, as a soul to live freely, and unimpeded to unfold such powers as were given her when we left our common home."[3]

Women not only spoke to the issue, they became more active; increasingly they insisted on being their own advocates. They secured entrée to more and more public activities: to municipal elections in 1869, to school boards in 1870, to the boards of guardians in 1875, to county council elections in 1888. They improved their legal position by getting laws passed giving them control of their earnings and property (1870), protecting the young girls among them from sexual offenses (1885), making the criteria for divorce more equal (1857 to 1923). They pried open the doors to hitherto masculine professions, particularly medicine and law, and forced the universities to accept them on equal terms.

Influential people were attracted to their cause: Benjamin Disraeli, John Stuart Mill, Harriet Martineau, Florence Nightingale, Jacob Bright, A. J. Balfour, George Meredith, Keir Hardie. Forceful leaders were found: Francis Power Cobbe, Josephine Butler, Mary Somerville, Lydia Becker, Mrs. Henry Fawcett, Emmeline Pankhurst. Notorious legal cases strengthened the position of women: the case of Caroline Norton, whose husband not only mistreated her and deprived her of her inherited wealth, but also of her earnings as a popular writer; the Clitherse case, in which a husband had abducted his wife and imprisoned her until she submitted to his demands; the conviction on a technicality of W. T. Stead, who, in his effort to halt the white slave traffic in young girls, showed by his own example how a girl of thirteen could be bought from her mother, kept in a brothel, and carried out of London. But despite all of these gains, one last prize was denied women, the right to vote for and hold parliamentary office.

One women's suffrage bill after another had been introduced in Parliament, but they all were voted down or, in the later stages of the struggle, defeated by stratagems. As the series of defeats accumulated, the acrimony of the debate increased, and as the government's position hardened, the actions of the Suffragists became more violent. In 1903 Mrs. Emmeline Pankhurst formed the Women's Social and Political Union, the organization responsible for most of the public agitation. In 1905 Suffragists began to interrupt public meetings which then led to a gradual increase in the scope and seriousness of their attacks on the government. In 1909 women imprisoned for political offenses began to hunger-strike in protest against the conditions in the prisons. The government reacted with forced feeding. Tempers heated and actions became more violent; the lines were drawn; a crisis seemed imminent.

V *Rebecca West as Feminist*

At this point in the Suffragists' campaign Rebecca West made her appearance. Converted while she was still in school, she and many of her fellow students had championed the feminine cause. They argued, they distributed pamphlets, they exposed them-selves to abuse of the kind she and her sister experienced when they were attacked by an old lady who, as she struck at them with her umbrella, exclaimed, "Thank God I am a womanly woman."[4] High spirited, ambitious, she despised the condescending discrimination of the male society about her. Possessing a mind alive with ideas and a pen quick to express them, she had no patience or desire to act the role of the reticent maiden waiting to be asked. Like Rebecca in Ibsen's *Rosmersholm* she responded to what she saw as the charged polarities of progress and reaction, but could recognize little that was neutral between them. As did Rebecca in the drama, she preferred to see herself as a free agent, a free thinker, and she championed the symbols of progress—individual freedom and social democracy. Perhaps most significantly, this young, vibrant aspirant believed her utopia could be achieved by argument, rational or polemic, and, as in the world of Ibsen's Rebecca, she accepted the assumption that newspapers could be used to fight the combat.

At any rate, so it happened. The actress became columnist and entered a period she later described as a "nightmare of overwork and harassment."[5] With that realization yet to come, she faced at the moment the challenge of making her way in London's literary life. She embraced this challenge as a feminist, assessing writers and their work from the view of an alert, responsive woman. Though her critiques were always alive with aesthetic values, entwined with them was another set of humanistic values: happiness, freedom, self-knowledge, self-realization, compassion, justice. As a feminist, she judged the literary work in part at least as an instrument of social reform.

To be a feminist was to be personally involved. The nature of the involvement might vary, but it was intense, an active assertion of individual conviction against the weight of society and its conventions. "I myself have never been able to find out precisely what Feminism is; I only know that people call me a Feminist whenever I express sentiments that differentiate me from a doormat or a prostitute."[6] This personal involvement meant fighting for the cause with the best means one had. It meant, too, an active commitment to experience, "a struggle of desire towards adventures whose nobility will fertilise the soul and lead to the conception of new, glorious things."[7] Wisdom was gained by letting one's sensibility respond to things outside one, by being "dependent for the value of this basis of wisdom on the extent to which we lean out of ourselves and adventure among alien things."[8]

Though the terms "good" and "bad" could be used, they were not the best terms for distinguishing the value of the experience because they were associated too closely with social and religious precedents which, to a member of a generation trying to shed the effects of Victorianism, were not accepted as salutary. Other terms seemed preferable, terms that were empirical, natural: "All that we know of morality is that it must be the kind of conduct that is instinctive to a healthy body; for if it conflicted a virtuous people would be doomed to extinction, which is absurd."[9] A healthy body would incorporate a nervous system strong and sensitive enough to perceive and comprehend the feelings of others, thus effecting a mutual sensibility that was to West the secret of virtue.

VI   *Men's View of Women*

She emphasized so forcefully the desirability of a freely given commitment because she saw everywhere about her evidences of stultifying inhibition and denial. Man was woman's most persistent tyrant and enemy; "there is something in the mind of humanity that turns again and again to anti-feminism, and I think it would be interesting if we inquired whether there is not in the mind of man a certain definite neurotic process which can be satisfied by nothing but definite and hostile measures against women. . . . Men are cruel to women. . .just as we are all cruel to our differences."[10] Women suffered most from men's jealousy because the legal, economic, and social systems favored men. Thus even an antifeminist writer like Harold Owen, whom West characterized as a "natural slave, having no conception of liberty nor any use of it,"[11] could assume a superiority over women.

The effect on women of this jealousy, West argued, was to put them in an ambiguous position; they were too good and yet not good enough. Women were expected to exemplify virtue. They were forced to practice an asceticism of thought, of conduct, of clothes, of food, not required of men. The activities that were given to these women fit the exigencies of the image which they had to exemplify, whether as student, as governess or school mistress, as nurse, as spinster. Even the rich woman, to whom society seemed to have offered everything and who was, in West's view, "the greatest luxury society has allowed itself,"[12] suffered an atrophy of the will and a corruption of the natural

sympathy she should have felt for her own sex. Society trained
her to value her sensations and her thoughts, but then forced her
to be idle. Finding no other outlet for her talents, she turned to
making herself attractive, to creating the alluring sex symbol
men wished her to be. Thus, West observed, "sex, which ought to
be an incident of life, is the obsession of the well-fed world."[13]
The obsession existed at the other end of the economic scale, too,
but there, because it took the form of prostitution, it degraded
socially as well as psychologically. Wherever she turned, West
found women hemmed in, restricted, sacrificed to men's
expectations. Even in their most accepted positions as wives and
mothers, women were expected to forgo the development of
their personalities for the sake of their husbands and their
children. Though they may be fit to vote and do other things men
did, they should not do them because all their energies were
supposed to be expended in the service of their families. Their
development, whatever there was of it, could be achieved only
in terms of what society demanded, not in terms of their own
potentialities.

Rebecca West found the answer to woman's dilemma where so
many other feminists found it, in individual freedom and
equality. She threw back in the faces of the men their argument
that women were inferior. Recognizing that women were
physically different from men, she denied that the difference
was a mark of inferiority. Weakness, as she defined it, was "the
sign of an organism ill-designed for its work."[14] To impute such
weakness to women was, she asserted, an impertinence. Man's
belief in his superiority had most obviously rested on his physical
strength. This she granted him. But to assume that man was also
mentally superior only excited her indignation; such an assumption was malignant and needed to be cauterized. Catching man
where he was emotionally weak, she shuddered with disdain,
"One shuns the company of the man who is convinced that his
mother was a fool."[15] She caught him also in his weakness for
idealizing the war-making male, or for creating other monuments
like the skyscrapers of New York City.

West went even further; she argued that whereas history
demonstrates woman's ability to maintain a consistent role for
herself as the attendant of men and children, men have turned
from their roles of hunting and farming to work instead with
machines and papers. The effect, she stated, is that man's

"primitive self is in conflict with his modern environment."[16] So, she argued, society should not choose as their leaders men like Winston Churchill and Napoleon who exude the kind of power admired in the past, but should choose instead married women who have maintained a consistent historical identity and have spent their lives in profitable political apprenticeships by teaching children moral behavior.

VII   *The Church and the Industrial Revolution*

Besides the conventional attitudes of men, Rebecca West listed two other sources of opposition to women's equality: the Church and the Industrial Revolution. The Church gave religious authority to many of the masculine assumptions about women. It could quote chapter and verse to prove that woman was subordinate to man and thus should love, honor, and obey in an ascending order of significance. Keeping the example of Eve before it, the Church had emphasized the sexuality of women. Either they enticed men into sin or they frigidly denied their own natural impulses. The Church fostered this self-denial, this inhibition, which, West argued, was an attrition of a great life force in humanity. She pointed out that it encouraged a double standard, requiring higher ethical conduct from women than from men and yet condoning a legal system that favored women not when they were at their best, but at their meanest or worst. To West it was a vile paradox that a woman who, from conviction, agitated for women's rights was more severely punished than a woman who ran her husband into debt or in a fit of viciousness threw vitriol in his face.

West saw the Industrial Revolution as an even greater barrier to the liberation of women. The owners of the factories and the mines preached and practiced the inferiority of women with a vengeance, not only the working class women, but the middle-class women as well. They forced the women of the working class into unhealthy, exhausting servitude, paying them only a fraction of what they paid the men. Women working under these conditions could not give birth to healthy children or care for them properly. When Professor Karl Pearson argued in the *Local Government Report of Infantile Mortality* that one should not reduce infant mortality because the high rate insured the survival of those most fit, West thought his assumption was

insane. She ended her attack on his report with the apostrophe:
"So before we kill the mothers in women by this unpleasant
present and that hopeless future, let us send out the capitalist to
fight the Angel of Death whom he called down to this massacre
of the innocents."[17]

The middle-class women faced a different problem; they
would have to stop their parasitic idleness and get out and work.
But if they did try to work they would need more than training;
they would have to effect a revolution in society, forcing it to let
them use their skills. The future of England, as West saw it,
offered two possibilities: either a progressive evolution of
gradual accommodation or a reactionary revolt returning England to the eighteenth century. The latter was the only
possibility if women were to be kept as parasites, but it meant too
that four-fifths of the population would be on a subsistence level.
With her argument so weighted, Rebecca West saw no choice.

The middle-class women did have the strength and means to
create and sustain the Suffragist movement. These women had
united in their effort, but despite their unity they could not bring
the working women into the struggle. To a degree the goals of
these two classes were different. However, like Sylvia
Pankhurst, the more gentle and lovable of the two Pankhurst
daughters, Rebecca West argued that the benefits of unity
transcended any differences the two groups may have had. The
strength of the middle-class woman was her education as well as
her relative security and independence; the strength of the
working woman came from her personal knowledge of society's
indifference and brutality, plus her truculence and her numbers.
Even the upper classes could furnish disciples, but they tended
to serve as symbolic rather than functional forces in the struggle.

West's sympathy was for the poor and disadvantaged. Though
she had the advantage of education and an inheritance of social
gentility, she had experienced what it meant to do the bleak,
bone-chilling labor of the poor and to feel the meager, stultifying
confinement of their lives. So she argued for the working women
from convictions born of her own experience. If as a feminist she
had a basic goal, it was to eradicate the conditions that
demoralized and weakened the working woman. West could see
that these women were already involved; they needed only to
activate their purpose. They were, she was convinced, a great,

unrealized asset in the feminine struggle for equality and freedom.

West's argument moved her far from the immediate demand for "Votes for Women," but she accomplished it with a display of energy and breadth of perception that the feminists of her day respected. She understood the needs of women as they were felt then and she could explain them within the context of the historical forces that had brought them and England to where they were. "Issues as grave as this are raised by feminism."[18]

VIII   *Reporting the Suffragist Struggle: 1912-13*

So runs the general argument through Rebecca West's feminist essays. To make this argument she would have needed only conviction, books, and seclusion to meditate on the problem. But she was there, in the midst of this feminist crisis in prewar Britain, and her record of these events often catches their excitement and vividness as they rushed by. Anyone familiar with the history of the Suffragist movement knows of the political meetings and the parades, the protest marches, the acts of violence and destruction of property, the great public spectacles organized by Mrs. Pankhurst and the Women's Social and Political Union, the machinations of the liberal party and Prime Minister Asquith, the arrests, the public trials, the imprisonments and hunger strikes and forcible feedings, the Cat and Mouse Bill, the raids on the WSPU headquarters and Christabel Pankhurst's flight to Paris, and then the great submersion of differences in the war effort, which finally secured women's suffrage. Rebecca West was there. She lived through the experience and helped make it what it was. Committed to the cause, but not to any one organization, she made her voice heard, weighted by her personal conviction and incisive intellect rather than the authority of Mrs. Pankhurst's WSPU, or Mrs. Fawcett's National Association, or that source of so much theoretical discussion, the Fabian Society, which had to be dragged reluctantly into this great national debate about women's rights. She advocated action and thus seems most attracted to those who act, particularly to Mrs. Pankhurst, for whom she had great admiration, but she kept her intellectual independence and a physical aloofness which put a distance between her and others, though it also assured her description of the events a clarity and verve that makes reading it a pleasure, despite the dusty hand of history which has long since shunted it under the accumulation of more recent years.

IX   *Emily Davison*

One example of her ability to capture these events is her eulogy to Emily Davison, the most revered martyr of the Suffragist movement. Other women died for their beliefs, but Emily Davison acted in her life and her death with a commitment and a view to capturing public attention that made her life and her death a heightened evidence of others' aspirations. The Suffragists had long realized that they could achieve their purpose only by gaining the public's interest. The WSPU in particular sensed the value of ritualistic spectacle. Its processions and pageants, its use of banners and badges and symbols of imprisonment and persecution captured the imagination of a usually indifferent, even hostile populace. The funeral of Emily Davison was such a spectacle, an event epitomizing the emotional quality of the Suffragist movement, a compound of sorrow and frustration and renewed dedication. The long parade of her funeral, the cortege with its coffin draped in a purple pall shot with the broad arrows taken from the Suffragist's prison costume, the women all dressed in white filing through the densely packed streets doing honor to one of their own, reveal to us something of the intense dedication these women felt for their cause.

Rebecca West, one of them, tried to put this feeling into her eulogy to Emily Davison. The funeral had taken place just days before. The need now was to summarize the meaning of the death and then rededicate oneself to the cause. Not many facts of Emily Davison's life were necessary, only those that demonstrated her unusual ability, her intelligence, her moral passion and dedication. She had, for example, secured what then would not have been easy to obtain, an exceptional education at Oxford and the University of London. Still, enough of a portrait of genteel ability was presented to serve as ironic contrast to the reality of her life as a Suffragist.

But for her last triumph, when in one moment, she, by leaving us, became the governor of our thoughts, she led a very ordinary life for a woman of her type and times. She was imprisoned eight times; she hunger-struck seven times; she was forcibly fed forty-nine times. That is the kind of life to which we dedicate our best and kindest and wittiest women; we take it for granted that they shall spend their kindness and their wits in ugly scuffles in dark cells.[19]

It is this life in prison which West emphasized, despite the fact that Emily Davison did not die there. But her will to martyrdom originated in Holloway Prison, where most of the arrested Suffragettes[20] were kept. Suffering from the horrors of a prison system that made no distinction between these political prisoners and conventional criminals, a decision by men in government that caused the Suffragettes to react with hunger strikes, she concluded that one great sacrifice might put an end to the tortures of her friends. Escaping her guard, she threw herself over the rail, but she suffered no serious injury. Determined to succeed, she climbed the stairs and jumped again. Again she failed to kill herself, though this time she injured her spine badly. This she did a year before her death. As much as life meant to her, she determined to end it in a way that would most affect the cause she believed in. Emily Davison killed herself by running in front of the horses racing at Ascot. She was struck by the horse ridden by the king's jockey.

Designating the government as the general enemy, West attacked those who sat at its center. She named them: Mr. McKenna, the home secretary, and Mr. Asquith, the prime minister, then described their villainy as compounded because, to prevent Mrs. Pankhurst, who was ill, from attending the funeral, they had arrested her. West saw the government's repressive obstinacy as evidence that the Suffragettes must do even more. They must demonstrate, they must convince the government that some people still object to the torture and murder of women. If the Government asks what it should do, it should be told that, to be free, women will do what they must, lawful or unlawful. If the Government cannot tolerate the resulting chaos, it can give women the right to vote.

Her sense of injustice and her anger carry her through more bitter, violent accusations to a final, high resolve:

Now that [Emily Davison] is laid to earth, will we break up the procession and melt into the wicked crowd? Or will we continue to follow in the hard path of tolerance and defense of a Cause that is fighting under extraordinarily difficult and perplexing conditions, till her spirit, eased by our achievements, may rest in peace, all being won?[21]

The youthful Rebecca West here makes clear her sense of identification with the militant Suffragette movement when it expressed, through heroines like Emily Davison, its determination to change an indifferent or hostile society.

X   *Venereal Disease*

But her belief in the cause was not slavish; she did not simply parrot doctrine from the headquarters of the various Suffragist societies. When Christabel Pankhurst wrote foolishly about prostitution and venereal disease,[22] West criticized her for her excess of spleen and lack of pertinent knowledge on the subject. "The real crime in Miss Pankhurst's article is her attitude towards those who suffer from sexual disease."[23] Pankhurst labeled all men as suspect, lacking the morality to be other than sexually promiscuous. To Rebecca West this was a crude simplification. Man lives in an environment that changes what should be the "bright glory of love"[24] into something that is "stale, unecstatic, grimy."[25] He is surrounded by contrived enticements, one "army of rich, parasite women who have nothing to do and no outlet for the force in them except to play with sex and make life its gaudy circus"[26] and another army of women who entice him to buy for a brief time all that they have to sell, their bodies. Guilt and innocence, West argued, is not so simple as Pankhurst had maintained.

But Pankhurst's attitude, West argued, caused even worse effects. Her hostility to the sufferer of disease intimidated him, made him fear to seek medical aid, and thus kept him as a source of infection of others. A society that accepted this attitude forced the expression of a fundamental human instinct into the very form Pankhurst found so repulsive.

For we have no Dionysiac festival, and where the human heart turns aside from the unsatisfying routine of modern industry it turns aside to no such clean orgy of riot and free-spent strength. Such adventurers must satisfy themselves with the poor glamour of the streets. If the woman goes out she must stay there always: and though the man comes back he is not less beggared.[27]

Which brings us to the heart of Rebecca West's argument. However right Pankhurst may have been in her abhorrence of venereal disease, she stated that abhorrence in attitudes no different from those held by the society that created them. She was a puritan among puritans. In contrast West argued a point of view that acknowledged the rightness of human instincts and asserted that their natural expression was both healthy and beautiful. "Much more powerful than moral enthusiasm is the disinclination of the immaculate flesh to risk the soilure of the streets. The body loves beautiful things. . .and the thing against which we are fighting is not a beautiful thing."[28] Activity characterized by beauty and health was West's answer to the inhibiting revulsion of Pankhurst, pity instead of scorn, an alternative instead of a condemnation.

XI   *Government Resistance*

But on the overriding principle of women's freedom they were in accord. Rebecca West was proud to have followed the Pankhursts in those great processions of Suffragists through the London streets. As they were united in that show of determination, they were united in their effort to push aside those forces which stood in their way. The most apparent obstacle was the government. Years before, this had meant the Conservative party, since by temperament this party was not amenable to change. When the Liberal party won the election of 1905, the hopes of the Suffragists rose because the new prime minister, Campbell-Bannerman, favored their cause. But he retired soon, and Asquith, who opposed woman's suffrage, became prime minister. The Suffragists began to attack him and his government as they had the Conservatives before. The most hated member of the cabinet was Home Secretary McKenna, who, through his control of the police and the prisons, could attack and punish the militant Suffragists at his discretion. His name was associated in their minds with police arrests and the Third Division in prison, with forced feeding and the Cat and Mouse Bill. One should expect, then, that West would attack him in her column.

One occasion has been noted already in the Emily Davison suicide. West found another occasion in his treatment of John Williams, a convicted murderer. Williams loved a young girl, Florence Seymour, and had gotten her with child. While he was in prison awaiting execution he learned of her condition and petitioned the home secretary to be allowed to marry her. McKenna denied his request. West's reaction? "Now, this is villainy."[29] First, it was the denial of a reasonable request from a man who, facing death, wished to rectify as best he could an act that would cause misery for one he loved. If this was not reason enough, then the fact that Florence Seymour, innocent of any crime for which John Williams was convicted, was being denied the security of marriage which her condition required. An unwed mother, she would become a social outcast. But most heinous of all, an innocent child would be denied legitimacy and a monetary legacy its father could give it. And so the injustice compounds, all because McKenna's "nonconformist conscience was ruffled."[30] "This new principle which holds that so long as we make a criminal smart it doesn't matter if we punish an innocent person at the same time, is most damnable."[31]

West was attacked in print for what she had written. One of her attackers described her as "a spiteful, unmarried female Church-woman brought up on the knees of curates."[32] Not cowed, she defended her position with effective arguments and facts, repeated that McKenna had misused his power, and disassociated herself from what was anathema to her, the pious meddling of the puritan conscience; "we have no right to stand between a human being and its desires unless they take the form of an attack on others."[33] Freedom, then, to do what one wishes, individual freedom and some measure of happiness are needed. She was well aware that we human beings are fallible, weak as well, and our lives too often are darkened by our own and others' mistakes, but this did not justify the government's using its power to compound the unhappiness and misery already too imminent for all of us. In her attack on McKenna and her demand for justice for Florence Seymour—which, in this imperfect world, was not to be had—Rebecca West makes the case not only for Florence Seymour, but for herself as well, and all that generation of women intent on breaking the bonds that government so insidiously and pervasively and invisibly had fashioned to hold them.

XII   *Emmeline Pankhurst*

In 1933, twenty years after the women's suffrage struggle had reached its climax and then was enveloped by World War I, Rebecca West recalled her impressions of the movement and its leader, Emmeline Pankhurst. Her portrait of Mrs. Pankhurst is sympathetic, stressing her "passion for the oppressed,"[34] her determination and courage to do and endure whatever was necessary to accomplish her goal, and, to paraphrase West's words, her stone-cold realism. Rebecca West saw Mrs. Pankhurst as a woman who learned not from books, but from experience. Though innately naive, she had grown to understand the quality of the opposition she was facing. History did teach her that concepts of justice and freedom which had been the clarion call of the French and American revolutions had now so developed in England that legions of women resented being hampered by arbitrary restrictions imposed merely on the basis of their sex. With equal certainty she learned from psychology that animus based in sex was so powerful in men that, if frankly expressed, it would cause women with any self-esteem to attack it. These two assumptions inform the principle in which she and the rest of the Suffragists believed: that democratic government must rest on the consent of the governed. On this principle her course of action could be built: withholding of consent to the actions of that government, disturbance of that government's orderly procedures, agitation for the franchise. Rebecca West accepts all of this. She sees as well that while they were needed, Mrs. Pankhurst and the Suffragette movement were indissoluble. When the need for the movement vanished with the passage of partial women's suffrage in 1917, Mrs. Pankhurst too disappeared, in part because she willed it, in part because England saw little need to remember the struggle. But Rebecca West understood her importance, both in her person and in her historical significance. Whatever her limitations, Emmeline Pankhurst was essentially glorious, and she would be remembered so in history.

As a force in history, her effect is described by West as

multiple. Looking back, West summarizes this determined woman's achievement, suffrage for women, so blandly that one senses how the urgency the author felt earlier is no longer there: "Few intelligent women in a position to compare the past with the present will deny the vote brought with it substantial benefits for women of both a material and spiritual kind."[35] Yet what a change this sentence encompasses. A second, more significant lesson West finds is that by her actions Mrs. Pankhurst forced the government to recognize finally that even she, a woman without high social influence, could make that government tremble if it did not heed her just requests. The result was a broadening of political power in England from which both men and women, particularly those of the lower classes, benefited. A third consequence West describes is more intriguing, paradoxical, and difficult to assess or explain. Let her state it.

But Mrs. Pankhurst's chief and most poignant value to the historian will be her demonstration of what happens to a great human being of action in a transition period. She was the last popular leader to act on inspiration derived from the principles of the French Revolution; she put her body and soul at the service of Liberty, Equality, and Fraternity, and earned a triumph for them. Then doubt seized her, as it was to seize a generation. In the midst of her battle for democracy she was obliged, lest that battle should be lost, to become a dictator. . . . She trembled under the strain of the conflict, and perhaps she trembled also because she foresaw that she was to gain a victory and then confront a mystery. . . . With her whole personality she enacted our perplexity, as earlier she had enacted our revolt, a priestess of the people.[36]

Mrs. Pankhurst epitomizes much that is of permanent interest to Rebecca West: an urgent need for social justice, a fascination with social change not so much for itself as for the effects it has on the people caught up in it, the force of an idea in action, the paradox of the individual at once so valuable and so insignificant. But for Rebecca West Mrs. Pankhurst was to be more admired than emulated. Whatever influence West exercised as a feminist, it did not result in public demonstrations. Her strength was rational argument. It moved from her mind to the printed page, and then into the public consciousness. Her virtue was an openness to experience, her gift a lively, articulate intelligence. Mrs. Pankhurst was the commanding general of the Suffragist movement. Rebecca West could be thought of as its herald and, to a degree, its historian.

XIII *Private Life*

Rebecca West pursued her public role as feminist primarily through her writing for the periodicals She was just as determined to realize her feminist ideals in her private life.[37] This meant that she intended to disregard as much as possible the inhibitive restrictions Victorianism was still able to impose on Edwardian women. Her early life was not sheltered, but it also was not an indoctrination into polite society. The families of both of her parents had distinction, but she found little opportunity to share it. The family life her father provided was intellectually stimulating and demanding, but he flawed it by his emotional instability. On her mother's side, her grandmother's runaway marriage to a talented musician who later distinguished himself helped create in the family a commitment to the values of the artist. Miss West and her two sisters inherited these interests and thus were motivated toward the professions and the arts. As a child living in poverty, she had little opportunity or desire to observe the social patterns of her school comrades. To them her behavior was odd and her clothes were shabby. The attacks of tuberculosis from which she suffered also forced her into solitary activities that left her with little inclination to worry about what ribbons were stylish that season, or how a young lady comported herself at the tea table, or even what the accepted rules of courtship were.

XIV *Early Relationship with H. G. Wells*

When Rebecca West came to London she was trying too hard to become an actress to build into that demanding regimen much semblance of a private life. When she was told by the administrator of the Royal Academy of Dramatic Arts, Kenneth Barnes, that she lacked what he called "personality" she turned with a similar intense energy to journalism. In September 1912 she reviewed in the *Freewoman* H. G. Wells's novel *Marriage,* accusing him of what he would have least expected, the literary prudishness of an old maid. This extraordinary attack caught his interest and he asked her to his country home, Little Easton

Rectory. For her, accepting this invitation involved a risk because his wife left him free to lead his emotional life where he wished. He had had a series of mistresses and at least one illegitimate child, but at this moment was emotionally not greatly involved with anyone. He and Rebecca West met with increasing frequency; the relation became intense, so intense indeed that in about June 1913 Wells broke with her. She was distraught, angry, suicidal, finding her salvation finally in projecting her turmoil into a series of three half-fictionalized articles — "Trees of Gold," "Nana," and "At Valladolid" — in which she thinly disguised her distress. The effect was salutary. She realized how close her violent emotions had brought her to self-destruction. She found in herself resources beyond anything she previously had realized: humor, reliance on art and work, a broadened perspective on the Suffragist cause. H. G. Wells read her new articles and saw that something had happened to her, that a new strength was there. He approached her again, offering her advice and friendship, which she at first resisted and then accepted. They became lovers, and on August 4, 1914, to the accompaniment of the news that England had declared war on Germany, she gave birth to their son, Anthony West.

XV   *Life of the Unwed Mother*

The presence of her son altered the character of her life. It meant for her the fabrication of a series of roles which would account for her small child and the coming and going of H. G. Wells. It meant her absenting herself from those places where her liaison with Wells would become too much a topic for public gossip. As a consequence she was forced into a lonely existence from which she could find little relief except in the visits of her lover. At times she was Mrs. West with a husband in cinematography or newspaper work, or she was Miss West caring for her nephew and Wells was a friend of the family. There were constant uprootings and changes of servants and members of the household, shuntings from Hunstanton to Braughing, from Alderton to Leigh-on-Sea, with rooms rented on Claverton Street in London if all else failed. Wells's visits fluctuated in relation to other demands made on him. Even when they went to the Continent she passed as his secretary or his companion. This was her life until late 1919, when she moved to Queen's Gate

Terrace, near Kensington Gardens in London, a move that was an attempt by her and Wells to make their relationship more public and, in the social group in which they moved, more acceptable. Still, this effort only mitigated somewhat the problems of her life. Everywhere there were too many disguises and make-dos, all of which were not in keeping with the image she had of herself as an emancipated women or even as a woman in love with a man who loved her. She always seemed to have to make the best of less, to realize that someone else had the better part of the bargain, even to suffer humiliation either from the public or from Wells himself.

XVI   *Deterioration of Relationship*

Rebecca West tried to continue her career, particularly as a reviewer of books, but the turmoil in which she lived made the steady effort of that work more demanding than she at times could manage. She had always taken pride in the speed with which she could accomplish a task, but this unstable, backstreet existence left her with little energy or peace of mind to achieve the professional aspirations she had. And if she could not work satisfactorily she had to do what was distasteful to her, depend on Wells for financial assistance.

There were quarrels, one over her concern for her son during German air raids on London, another about Wells's infidelity with Maxim Gorky's secretary, another created by Wells's unwarranted jealousy of her. Their relationship became strained. It reached a crisis when, in March 1923, as she was planning a lecture tour in the United States, she was warned that an effort would be made to hold her at Ellis Island because of her "immoral" relation with Wells. She had wanted Wells to marry her. Faced with this threat she became more insistent, even to the point of insisting that either he would marry her or they would have to sever their relationship. The distance grew between them. If the opportunity had come, she still would have married him, but it never did. Of importance too was the fact that Wells was passing into old age, which meant that some of the control of the relationship was slipping from Wells to Rebecca West. For years he had largely dictated the conditions of their life together, but as he passed into his fifties with his health becoming more uncertain, and she moved into her late twenties with the accumulating responsibilities of her son's education, he became more emotionally dependent on her. Another crisis occurred. In June 1923 a woman with whom Wells had been intimate tried to commit suicide in his apartment. The potential for scandal was great for both Rebecca West and Wells. When, as a result, she showed even greater determination to break with him, he threatened to take her son away from her. She used her delayed American tour, which began in October, to help establish some greater independence. Gradually the separation stabilized.

XVII End of Relationship

In this final phase of their relationship, their son, Anthony, became increasingly the interest that kept a mutual tension alive. His parents argued about his schooling; both of them were convinced as to the value of education, but they disagreed about its characteristics. As would a divorced couple, they sought to establish legal assurances of their son's financial security. In 1928 the boy fell ill; the diagnosis was tuberculosis, the disease from which his mother had suffered as a young girl, leaving her with a damaged lung and a tendency to relapse into a phthistic condition. Though this diagnosis later proved to be wrong, the patient's mother worried through six months of this illness; it is not so evident that Wells did. But this illness, plus West's critical treatment of Wells's work in her collection of literary criticism, *The Strange Necessity,* that appeared at the same time, caused Wells to assume proprietary interests over his son, even to the extent of blocking Rebecca West's efforts to legitimize in the courts her relations with her son. Anthony's father began inviting him to his home for vacations and the boy was made to feel he should make choices between his parents, causing bitterness among all three of them.

XVIII Marriage to H. M. Andrews

In 1930 Rebecca West made a formal break from Wells by marrying Henry Maxwell Andrews. Mr. Andrews brought order and contentment back into her life. A description of that marital relationship is to be found in *Black Lamb and Grey Falcon,* where he appears as a stabilizing, calming influence on her, secure in his opinions, never appearing to be intimidated by her quick, cutting intelligence, but also not overbearing. On her side she seems often deferential, respectful. Between the two of them flows a warmth and understanding that does not seem to be strained by the abrasions and constant intimacy of that long, sometimes difficult journey through Yugoslavia. For most of this marriage Rebecca West lived with her husband in the rural quiet of Ibstone House, near the village of High Wycombe in the Chiltern Hills.

To discuss West's private life in feminist terms requires the recognition that she did pursue the life of the heart without the sanction of society wherever her heart led her. She made what compromises she felt she had to make. She did flinch from the pain her situation caused her, but basically she was constant to her purpose. Whether the feminist prerogatives of her private life should have taken precedence over the feminist prerogatives of her professional career can only be answered if one is willing to recognize the harsher social prescriptions of that period and the inescapable physiological fact that it was she who must give birth to the son whom she and H. G. Wells conceived. That she did not give up the child is a mark of her strength. That she did not simply lapse into a captive domesticity is also a display of her will and her belief in her own genius. And that she did produce six books and hundreds of reviews and other pieces of writing during this period speaks well for her professional commitment. No one has found the perfect solution to the essential paradox a woman who wishes everything both a private and a professional life can give her must face. She cannot preserve the smooth continuity ideal to either aspect of her life. She can perhaps achieve an equitable solution to the conflicts that the exigencies of two concurrent professional careers, hers and his, can cause. West did not find that equity, but it is hard to conceive how she could have. The imbalance with which the relationship began was not so much the differing expectations of a male and a female as it was that of one career being at its apex while the other was only beginning. If feminism can be thought of simply as a woman's belief in her own worth, then Rebecca West's experiences with H. G. Wells seem justified. One need only set the shrill audacity of her early Suffragist writings against the considered feminine wisdom of her essay "Uncle Bennett," in which she attempts to summarize her opinion of Wells as author, written as it is at the conclusion of her close relationship with him, to realize the progress that experience had effected.

CHAPTER 2

Critic and Reviewer of Books

I *Reputation*

REBECCA West has reviewed books almost all of her professional life. Not only does she seem to have had her say about everyone of her own generation with any literary pretensions, but she has read libraries of the literature of the Western world, from the patristic fathers to the most recent best sellers, and has commented at least in passing on most of her reading. In its mass and its display of thought and originality, this performance constitutes one of the substantial sources of her literary fame.

She came by this fame quickly. Before she was thirty she had produced a series of reviews that Frank Swinnerton described, in his literary history of the period, as a model of excellence.

I doubt whether any such brilliant reviews of novels were ever seen before; they certainly have not been seen since, for when Rebecca West left the *New Statesman* her peculiar combination of wit could not be replaced. Those who read novel reviews are thankful if they find either wit or justice in them, and the difficulty of writing any form of criticism which is sensitive to the aims of authors and at the same time inexorable in appraisal of their performance is extreme. This difficulty, commonly evaded by means of impudence or disingenousness, Rebecca West mastered. She amused, she stung; but she held fast to her own standard of quality, and was just.[1]

From Swinnerton this is praise indeed. But what seems to be justice to one may not appear so to another. Rebecca West has a reputation for outspoken frankness that causes some to fear her and others to react in anger, as Evelyn Waugh did in one notable instance. When her comments are more muted they still can have a sharpness that make some of her acquaintances wary of her.

37

Ethel Mannin, for example, who knew her socially, felt uneasy
with her and tried to describe why in her autobiography.

Rebecca West was there, vivid and vivacious as always, and as usual
being amusing at someone else's expense. She is a brilliant mimic, but
with her one can never feel quite comfortable; there is always the
feeling that when one has left the room she will be as amusing about
oneself. . . .
   In appearance she is small and provocative, rather like a lovely
naughty child, with her flashing gipsy eyes and her shining black hair.
There is always a sort of mockery in her eyes and about her
mouth. . . . Admiring her in so many ways, her looks, her wit, her
intellect, her vivacity, I wish I knew her really well—but she is not easy
to know, and she appears to dislike more people than she likes. She has
a mind like a sword-blade, and a tongue like a whip. I feel that she
would have to like and admire and respect one very much indeed
before one could ever hope to get close to her.[2]

   Hugh Walpole feared her. When she reviewed his novel *The
Dark Forest* he incautiously wrote to her, accusing her of having
"one more dig" at him. She responded:

I suggest that this talk about my "continuing for ever and ever this
public scalping" is literary gossip without any basis in fact. I do not
conceal my feelings when I think people are talking nonsense, and I
have practised this candour over Ellen Key and Mrs. Humphrey Ward
and Strindberg.[3]

She goes on to state that she is equally candid when she likes
someone's work, but this offered no consolation to Walpole, nor
would it to many others who have felt the sting of her criticism.
Walpole confided to Frank Swinnerton that he wished she would
elope with another reviewer whose "sublime patronage" irri-
tated him almost as much as that of Rebecca West, and that their
boat would "sink crossing the Channel!"[4] Even when one is just a
reader of Rebecca West's work, one senses in her a desire to
keep her distance and maintain relations with others as much as
possible on her own terms.
   But none of this seems to have handicapped her in her work.
Her abilities were respected by the publishers and editors. They
gave her as much work as she seems to have been able to do. The
books came in; she curled up in bed to read them, two and three

at a time; she wrote the reviews and saw them published. The effort was demanding, but she was proud of her ability to do it quickly and efficiently, despite the frustration and overwork that sometimes made it burdensome. She was what she expected any woman in her position to be, a professional.

II *Résumé of Career*

A listing of her reviews is impressive. In number they approach a thousand. Since usually they were done on assignment, they appear in series in specific time periods and in specific journals and newspapers. Her format for these reviews may vary, but within a series it remains relatively constant. The principal series are as follows.

In February 1912 she began her career typically with an attack on that formidable defender of the Establishment, Mrs. Humphrey Ward, in the avant-garde, feminist the *Freewoman*. She continued this series in like tone through much of that year. When the *Freewoman* stopped publication for lack of popular support, West moved in September 1912 to the *Clarion,* though she continued as an editor on the staff of the *Egoist,* a publication Dora Marsden, the editor of the *Freewoman,* had set up to replace it. In the *Clarion* Rebecca West mixed book reviews with reports of current events. The series is emotional, even intemperate, but it is full of her observant reporting of this emotion-charged period in British history. In January 1915 she returned to literary reviewing in the *London Daily News,* a series that lasted over five years. The books she reviewed make up a grabbag of fiction and nonfiction in which the only common interests apparent are feminism and politics. As would be inevitable, the quality of the literature she reviewed is uneven and most of it has drifted into obscurity. A few reviews of authors with the stature of James, Bennett, and Hardy could be salvaged.

In 1919 she wrote a short series of dramatic reviews in *Outlook, London* and continued the same topic in another short series, entitled "The Theatre," in *Time and Tide.* She found British theater of this period dull, so her reviews are charac- terized by various diversions in which she gives us glimpses into the workings of the theatrical world, the function of the set designer, for example, or she reminisces on past experiences, like her memories of being caught up by the magic of Sarah

Bernhardt. These are subjects that meant more to her than the ostensible occasion for her review, but they are also only tangential to what should be her central concern, the drama she had seen. Whether her interest in drama waned since that earlier time when she had thought to make it her career, or the circumstances of this kind of criticism made uncongenial demands of her, she did not write another series of dramatic reviews in the rest of her long career. However, her relationship with *Time and Tide* did not stop when whe wrote her last column for "The Theatre." For over thirty years she continued to serve as a director and occasional contributor to this periodical.

In 1920 she began the series of reviews that impressed Frank Swinnerton so much. The series, entitled "Notes on Novels," appeared in the *New Statesman*. The success of this series is even more remarkable when one realizes that West later characterized the period in which they were produced as lost, for literature, "except for a few isolated books, written out of a powerful preoccupation,"[5] and that not many of even those few books appear in her reviews. Each "note" presented two or three novels, usually related by some common topic, that interested West greatly; the possibilities of the topic she would then explore in a series of reviews. She did this when she analyzed why some contemporary novelists, Katherine Mansfield and Brett Young among them, wrote in a prose style bordering on poetry. She could do the same for possible origins of a style, or of cultural and historical contexts, and even on occasion she would ride her old hobbyhorse feminism, not as a cause, necessarily, but as an interest in how the feminine sensibility expressed itself in fiction. This last topic she could hardly have avoided if she had wanted to because of the abundance of women novelists then at work. The list includes Rose Macaulay, Katherine Mansfield, and, of course, Virginia Woolf. Woolf particularly stands out, for she is the only author in this list to whom West looks with genuine awe and admiration.

West's tendency is to discuss an author at least as much as his work, which makes her "old-fashioned" as a critic, but it also is one of her strengths, for it gives these reviews much of the bite and interest they have. Criticism of this kind is dependent on accumulated reading and a retentive memory. These characteristics begin to appear in this series, giving her increasingly the general view, the knowledge and judgment to present a conclusive summation of each of the authors. What Walpole complained about as "sublime patronage" and another writer objected to as her pontifical tone could, with greater objectivity, be accepted as the expression of a well stocked mind and a straightforward commitment to aesthetic and intellectual criteria that enabled her to view the latest Walpole production in a larger context and find it and him wanting.

"Notes on Novels" ended in 1922. During the next four years Rebecca West published little. In part this lapse was caused by a lecture tour in the United States she made during 1923–24. Though the tour was not as successful as she had hoped, it gave her the opportunity to make friends, mostly in the New York literary world, and to establish relations with American publishers, particularly the *New York Herald Tribune*, for which she agreed to provide a series of literary essays. A proviso of the contract required her to come to America twice each year to aid in the preparation of the series. One effect this continued contact with America had was that with increasing frequency she published her work in American journals and newspapers.

The series she wrote for the *Herald Tribune* was published between October 1926 and February 1932. Its importance cannot be minimized, for in it West brought her concept of the book review to its culmination. Some of the credit for this achievement must be given to the *Herald Tribune* because it provided her with encouragement, sufficient time, and ample space, all of which helped her realize her potential. The rest of the credit is hers. Choosing her subjects more carefully than is apparent in her other series, she presented a gallery of literary portraits that stand today as her definitive statements on many of these writers. She began by choosing more American topics than British, but gradually shifted back to those British authors she knew best: Bennett, Galsworthy, Shaw, Woolf. She thought well enough of some of these portraits to collect them in her book *The Strange Necessity* (1929).

During part of this same six-year period, from July 1928 to June 1930, she wrote a series of more impressionistic sketches of the current cultural scene which she published in the *Bookman* and then partially collected in the book *Ending in Earnest* (1931). She thought of these sketches as letters, labeling them "A Letter from London" or "A Letter from Abroad." She kept the form of these sketches loose and casual, mixing her literary topics with descriptions of where she was and what she was doing. A pleasing blend of travel sketch and literary review, this form could be termed a variant of that kind of personal, impressionistic reaction between traveler and place that, in commenting on Kipling's travel book *Land and Sea,* she described as *le grand reportage.*

The most casual, most personal, and least rewarding of this drift toward off-the-top-of-the-head, itinerant reporting and reviewing is the series, captioned "I Said to Myself," that West wrote between June 1931 and May 1933 for Hearst's *New York American.* Her contribution was part of an unsuccessful campaign to improve the ailing newspaper's circulation. During about the same period (December 1931 to January 1934) she returned to more conventional book reviewing for the *London Daily Telegraph.* This was reviewing books with a vengeance, because she covered five or six books in each essay. The listings of the books reviewed suggest little evidence of selection; they are of all kinds and all degrees of excellence. When this series ended, her work as a reviewer almost stopped until after World War II.

The book reviewing she has done since the war has been mainly for two London newspapers, the *Sunday Times* and the *Daily Telegraph,* but these reviews increasingly are of biographies and histories. This shift of interest, she has said, was caused by her concern for the deteriorating state of western civilization, a concern that appeared increasingly as a theme in her reviews in the 1930s and persisted long into the post-World War II period. She attempted to summarize her thinking about literature and society in the Terry Lectures she gave at Yale University in 1957, published later under the title *The Court and the Castle.* The theme she chose for these lectures was the individual's relation to authority and the gradual alienation and dehumanization of the individual in that relationship. This theme is congenial with the view of history she had been developing since the 1930s.

The aggressive enthusiasm for change of the young Rebecca West has turned in her later years to no more than a guarded holding on to those more persistent qualities she sees as simply supportive of life. To say that her reading of books and making public her thought on that reading are solely responsible for this change would be to exaggerate the importance of that reading. But the reading did play its part. More than most people,

Rebecca West has looked to books for answers, and again more than most, she has told us the answers she has found.

III   *Critical Criteria: Style*

Rebecca West wrote in the epilogue to *Black Lamb and Grey Falcon* that she had discouraged a student from attempting a thorough study of her work because it had not been intended as a continuous, integrated presentation of her views or personality. Her purpose, she argued, was the quite different one of discovering for her own enlightenment what she had learned about various subjects. Though one might grant her this demurral, one still can assume, when it is limited to her interest in literature, that certain preferences and predilections will emerge, and to that extent unify her presentation.

Like any other critic, she insists first that the author use language in a pleasing manner. West does not define her preferences narrowly; style, for her, can be as various as the flowers of the field and garden, and can offer as many fragrances. Certainly she recognizes differences of degree, because the impulse to seek for that which makes for distinctiveness appears on almost every page of her critical essays. But her search is not based on standard a priori critical assumptions, or the dicta of any particular school of criticism. Instead, she quoted with approval the neoclassical writer Maurras, whose dying advice to his friends was to stop troubling themselves "about romanticism and classicism and to think a little more about the difference between good and bad writing."[6] Good and bad writing, the skill with which the author uses his medium to achieve his end, this is what initially interests West most. That end can become complicated later by her concern about how art serves life, but initially she judges skill.

Her own style is, for the most part, rich, allusive, vigorous, its substance the outflow of a retentive, abundant memory and a mind alert to the significance and relatedness of things, its energy created primarily by her impulse to explain, evaluate, and argue, its strength the force of her conviction and the power of her argument. When it is less than its best, it falters because she seems to begin saying, "I'm right because I'm right," and adopts an uncharacteristic shrillness, or she loses her energetic stride and begins to mince, exclaiming with too much gesture and niceness of tone over some beauty she has just perceived.

But she does not let her personal predilections with words get in the way of her ability to appreciate the use other authors make of language, though the styles they use are as different as Twain's American colloquial creation, with its careful attention to local dialect and rhythm, or Yeats's prose, languorous and elegant, in which a sentence "would have the distinguished air of a long, ringed, white hand in an old picture."[7] She can enjoy styles as different as these and still find pleasure in the style, different again, of Willa Cather, who "builds her imagined world almost as solidly as our five senses build the universe around us."[8] As she evaluates them, each of these styles is recognized as having its own shape and color, its own unity and integrity. Each style demonstrates, too, a respect for its common source, the English language. Each is equal to the burden its creator expects it to carry.

An inadequate style can be fatal. To West it means confusion, or triteness, or a lack of independence, or simply thoughtlessness, this last being as damning a judgment as she can make. Those authors who came under her critical lash for their inept use of language make a strange collection, among them Balzac, whose style at times "goes all to pieces with its own ardour, like a guttering and smoking candle in need of snuffing,"[9] Wells, whose writing suddenly "loses its firmness and begins to shake like a blanc-mange,"[10] Alec Waugh, whose prose gave West the feeling of "getting lost in the corridors of a tube station,"[11] and Hall Caine, whose style repelled her by its "peculiar violent idiocy."[12] Of course Balzac and Wells, in West's judgment, transcended their limited technical abilities to create beautiful structures of words; Waugh and Caine did not. Style remains one important means of making a judgment.

IV   Critical Criteria: Vulgarity and Sentimentality

When West goes beyond the evaluation of technical skill to examine the quality of the author's mind, she impresses the reader as simply bristling with distinctions, ranging all the way from the immediate purposes an author may have for writing a best seller to the ultimate ends of life itself. For the most part her distinctions tend to exclude, to measure the example at hand against those ultimate ends and find it wanting. Innately high-minded and fastidious, West is a seeker of what she discerns as manifestations of excellence, of the best that humanity can be or do.

When it is less than that, when it seems vulgar, for example, she reacts with what appears to be an instinctive revulsion. Vulgarity in its most commonly understood form, as she finds it, for example, in the drama presented at the Grand Guignol, with its mixture of prurience and sadism, or in Faulkner's novel *Sanctuary*, with its similarly indecent elements, makes her draw away in disgust. The grosser parts of Joyce's fictive world, his use of obscenities, his absorption in the facts of Dublin squalor, his fascination with the functions of the body, its excrements and fatty effluvia, cause her again to draw back, though in this instance she can make a distinction, since some of this same interest, as expressed by D. H. Lawrence with more sanctity and higher purpose, she can note with qualified approval.

That which is vulgar in the more radical sense, of the *vulgus*, makes her react as would a woman of genteel background, though the sources of her reaction are talent and taste, not the mindless acquired prejudice of a social class. She works at being fastidious. She wants to know, to understand; making distinctions of this kind becomes a means of gaining that understanding. For her, pedestrianism is vulgar in its thoughtless diligence; riding the Tosh-horse (the writing of best sellers), with its blend of sincerity and vitality, is also vulgar. All such efforts smack too much to Rebecca West of senseless drudgery, of uninformed dullness, of muddled forms and muddied thought. In her judgment an artist who produces this kind of work is not true to himself or to his art.

The artist who is too willing to attune his work to what he thinks the public wants earns another epithet from West. He is sentimental. He has eyes and ears, and he can make intelligent use of what he sees and hears, but he has committed himself to play by rules subject to the shifts of intellectual and social currents that he may or may not understand. He is a puppet moving to the tugs of his audience. This may not be what we recognize as an orthodox characterization of the sentimental artist, yet it permits West to point to that which she disapproves of in many modern writers, a self-conscious catering to one's audience. Whether it is seen as vulgar or sentimental, it is, in her view, the artist playing a false game with his genius.

V   Critical Criteria: Art and Reality

The artist more apt to win West's respect must show in his work that he has great understanding of himself, the world he lives in, and his relation to that world. She respects H. M. Tomlinson, a writer of remarkable travel books, because "by naming things rightly he creates them,"[13] which he can do with what she judges to be an easy, erudite self-awareness. She can accept as well another approach to reality, that of a self-effacing reconstitution of memory, as she found it in the fiction of Marcel Proust, since his method also resulted in a valid artistic presentation of the reality he knew. What both authors display is a lively intelligence actively engaged with the matter at hand. If one becomes obsessively single-minded about that matter at hand, as West noted of "the orgiastic fantasy of Burns and the necrophilic fantasy of Poe,"[14] then one is diminished thereby. But even these artists are still eager, engaged, and still partake of that greatness which West finds more completely realized by the artist who is open to more experience, a Balzac, who planned to put all France into 300 novels, or a Goethe, who is ubiquitous in his "scouting on every frontier of the collective intelligence."[15] But they all have in common an aware, eager engagement with the facts of their worlds, and that engagement results in a kind of truth Rebecca West respects. In her stressing, as she does, the artist's effective relation with his world, Rebecca West sets down in empiricism one philosophical anchor for her theory of art, an anchor emphasized by her critic and admirer Evelyn Hutchinson.[16]

But to Rebecca West it is not enough to be like Stendhal's mirror ambling down a highway. For her the great artist is one who also engages in an act of discovery, for himself, and for his reader. Great art is an exploration as well as an explanation. The artist's search takes him to the vanguard of his age and culture, and then pushes both himself and his readers a little beyond. Viewing art in this way, as a source of society's advancement, West allies the artist, at least in purpose, with that other explorer on the forward edge of knowledge in whom H. G. Wells puts so much trust, the scientist. The scientist helps create his future. The artist, by an act of wisdom, foretells his.

The greatest art is ultimately, in the terms West most often reiterates, an affirmation of life over death. In their simplest sense these terms mean that being is better than not being, though it may be no more than the sluttish life lived in a Dublin back-bedroom by Joyce's Molly Bloom. In its more significant aspect, life is a conscious, sentient realization of what being means. Art can be the form that knowing, that realization, takes. To Rebecca West, both creating great literature and reading it are continually a series of enlightenments that "[t]his much we now know."[17] "The thing has been done, the absolute truth about that situation has been set down, we are by that much more completely masters of reality than we were."[18] It is this kind of understanding, this kind of quasi-religious using of intelligence for goodly purposes, that we can sense Rebecca West striving for in her best work as a reviewer of books. Thus the high standard against which she finds so few can measure up, and thus the disappointment she so often registers in her record of her search.

The cumulative effect of this high purpose one senses in reading her reviews is not unlike that which one receives from reading the essays of Matthew Arnold, for they both assume that art has great social significance, they both have set high their standards for evaluating that art, and both assume that they are instruments of enlightenment and uplift for their readers, the public. Rebecca West might be surprised to find herself compared to a pillar of that Victorian Establishment she opposed so violently when she was young and felt its weight most sharply, but though times may change, she would be the first to recognize that the roles we may select to play do not. She has not lived all these years with the name she chose to make her own, Rebecca West, without an awareness of the public responsibility that name carries with it.

In summary, she values the individual insight, and she prefers to relate the work to its author and the cultural forces that influenced him. The admiration she expresses for the imagination, the flash of insight, would prevent her from making any abiding commitment to a methodology insistent on separating the work from its creator, or stricter in its delimitation of the area of investigation, or overly absorbed in the minutiae of the work, or strongly dependent on a canon of received dogma. If we

place her among the critics for whom she feels affinity, the list
would include Lamb, Hazlitt and DeQuincey, Lessing and St.
Beuve, Leslie Stephen, George Moore, and Paul Valéry. The
work of these critics is impressive, but it has not enjoyed great
vogue in West's lifetime. It helps explain her preference among
her contemporaries for an Edmund Wilson to an F. R. Leavis or a
Paul Elmer More.

VI   Henry James

Rebecca West has collected her views on literature in four
books and a monograph: *Henry James* (1916), *The Strange
Necessity* (1928), her *Elegy* for D. H. Lawrence (1930), *Ending in
Earnest* (1931), and *The Court and the Castle* (1957). She wrote
Henry James early in her career, making it her first major effort
at literary criticism. That she would publish this study of Henry
James in 1916, the year of his death, is both unexpected and
commendatory. It is unexpected for two reasons. James's
popularity had dwindled for a long time until as an old man he
was ignored by all but a few who still accepted him as the
"master." Then also, H. G. Wells, with whom West was so
intimate both as lover and literary colleague, was in many
respects the outspoken antithesis of James. For her to write this
critical study, which is in effect to defy the public's neglect of
James and tacitly to contradict Wells, who cleverly, crassly, and
without forewarning had lampooned James in his book *Boon,*
speaks well for her straightforward independence as a critic.

But she would not have written the study simply out of pity or
defiance. She admired James's work. She saw in him a stylist who
valued the qualities of words. She respected his effort to correct
by example and precept what he considered to be the
carelessness and vulgar excesses of the Victorians. A craftsman,
he displayed in his stories a technical virtuosity that prompted
her to praise them as "exquisite vessels that swaggeringly hold
and clearly show the contained draught of truth,"[19] a statement
that should be read as praise of James in a clever imitation of
James's own style. An advocate of the new realism, James showed
a special sensitivity for those psychological subtleties in individuals that West presented in her own fiction. In part, West was
attracted to James as a person for the same reason, because she

saw in him what he would have called a "special case," a unique product of a unique moment in American history, who was actively trying to determine what that uniqueness meant. She found in him, as well, a model of the artist who possesses that special prophetic vision, that sense of having a special mission, a sacred vocation.

This is not to say that West found no faults in the "Old Master." He was too much given, she thought, to standing aside and observing the active world, to sensating rather than acting. Also, despite his fascinated devotion to things from the past, he seemed insensitive to the fact that these beautiful things could have been created in times that were just as painful to those living in them as any he could have known. West can explain this failure—"One perceives with relief that he said these things because, as one guessed in *The Passionate Pilgrim,* his strong sight of the thing that is was accompanied by blindness to the thing that has been"[20]—but she cannot forgive it. She, the European, realizes more acutely the cost her ancestors paid in happiness and life to bring these beautiful things into existence than does the American James. In her view, he was unable also to grasp the large philosophical and political problems of his own time, and when he attempted them in his fiction, his manner seemed ponderous and out of proportion to the result he attained. Her criticism here, though, is tempered when compared to Wells's clever but brutal censure of James's work as resembling a church in whose center stood highlighted an altar displaying a dead kitten, an eggshell, and a piece of string.

Even today, after the avalanche of Jamesian criticism we have experienced since World War II, West's pioneer study of Henry James has a freshness that makes it interesting reading. Her judgments often have been supported by later critics; when they have not, the reader is put to it to refute her argument. She anticipates to a degree Van Wyck Brooks's thesis that James's lack of identification with American culture had a debilitating effect on his fiction, but without the factitious chauvinism of Van Wyck Brooks's interpretation. She favors James's earlier, simpler fiction, so she would disagree with F. O. Matthiessen in his defense of the later "major phase." In all, she paid a fine tribute to James at a time when it took courage and critical perception to do so.

VII   *"The Strange Necessity"*

The book *The Strange Necessity* consists of one long essay and eleven short essays. The long essay, also titled "The Strange Necessity," is published here for the first time. The rest of the book consists of essays West culled from the series she wrote for the *New York Herald Tribune,* plus one essay from the *New Statesman.* The topic of the long essay is the nature of art; the subject of the short essays circle about this same topic. This collection of essays represents the end of a phase in West's professional life. They comprise her attempt to summarize her thinking about literature, her conclusions drawn from sixteen years of writing book reviews.

The lead essay is not a treatise; rather, it is an unusual combination of impression and argument by analogy. In it West tries to weave her impressions of a day in Paris with her thoughts about Joyce, Constant, and Proust, and how their art relates to the scientific findings of Professor. Pavlov as recorded in his book *Conditioned Reflexes.* If West had wished to stress the dominant motif of her essay, she could have titled it "Correspondences": art corresponds to life, the artistic reflexes of Joyce and Proust and West herself correspond to the hunger reflexes of Pavlov's dogs, the method of the artist corresponds in some basic ways to the method of the scientist, West's use of one day as the frame for her essay corresponds with Joyce's similar use of one day in *Ulysses,* her method of relating actual existence with the life of the mind has correspondences with Joyce's narrative method in *Ulysses.* If all these correspondences were not enough, West also makes her presentation an important dimension of her own argument. The effect of this effort at establishing correspondences is to create a sense of inclusiveness, of making everything relate to everything else. Art is not something separate, an activity specialized, uniquely human, the interest of a certain temperament. It is related to everything we do, it is a necessity.

Considering the use West makes here of Pavlov's scientific interests, one can see this essay as evidence of the intellectual influence of H. G. Wells on Rebecca West. Just as Wells tried to impose the biological model on history, so West here argues its relevance to what conventionally would be thought of as a less amenable human activity, the creation of art. One can read this essay as a daring attempt to explore the possibilities of scientific humanism. As West presents them, both art and science are means of effecting understanding and have many characteristics in common. Her intent in this essay, however, is one sided, for in it she tries to demonstrate how the scientist can enlighten the artist about the artist's métier.

The thesis West develops is that basically art satisfies our desire to know. She accepts beauty as a concept, but she is not so much interested in the particular qualities it may have as she is in the effect it has on the human organism. Her emphasis is psychological, one might even say physiological, for much of the argument she develops centers on the analogies she can draw between what she understands our response to art to be and her understanding of Pavlov's experiments on the conditioned reflexes of dogs. Accepting Pavlov's argument that the basis of behavior is the reflex and, on the suggestion of Pavlov and Herbert Spencer, enlarging the term *reflex* to include certain reactions of the whole organism, reactions more conventionally identified by the term *instinct,* West saw in this perception a justification for art within concepts that are in accord with a scientifically oriented society. Pavlov argued that freedom was such a reflex or instinct. West argued by analogy that another reflex equally basic to humanity was what she called the investigatory or "What-is-it" reflex.

The activity of this investigatory reflex is to collect information and to arrange it into significant patterns. As West states it in what for her is uncharacteristic jargon, it is a process "of analysis and synthesis of experience terminating in the creation of excitatory complexes."[21] Everyone engages in this process of analysis and synthesis all his life. At first he has little to work with and thus synthesizes patterns that are false and self-serving. The urgent psychic need he feels for something permanent forces him to construct these patterns in his infancy, a time when he has no information that could refute them, and to cling to them unconsciously through the rest of his life. These patterns, this fantasy, as West calls it, is a constant against which their possessor in later life must always match reality. The method used for establishing this correspondence varies with the individual. Some people work out their fantasies in actions, others are more absorbed in their contemplation of these fantasies, still others prefer to create artifacts of their concept of reality. Artists comprise this last group.

As do we all, the artist has the problem of maintaining a fine balance between his fantasy of the world and the reality of the world his senses and reason convey to him. If his fantasy dominates, he risks the taint of sentimentality; if reality prevails, he may produce only a copy of that reality. The greater and more prevalent danger is the tendency toward sentimentality. If, however, the artist does his work well, then we who view that work see in it a pattern induced by the fantasy of the artist yet also correspondent with reality. His creation becomes so uniquely revelatory of that reality, so well done, so truthful, that we, the readers, also can comprehend that reality.

West is not satisfied to limit the value of art to its effect on individuals. She returns to Pavlov and his concept of the mind, the cortex, as an analyzing and synthesizing mechanism which can integrate units into an excitatory complex, and sees there the possibility of enlarging the function of the work of art. As the mind accumulates its findings, so does art, the one internal, individual, the other external, possessed by all those who are aware of it. Art becomes what West calls a "super-cortex," created out of its own necessity, external to man, a means of examining the most complicated forms of experience, and perhaps most beneficial to its creator, capable of storing its formulae of those experiences, of repeating them, of making them available when asked for. A "brain" outside the brain, it is not so subject to the hazards and limitations encountered by the individual human being.

West's logic has brought her here to the point where she, who once had the reputation of being an iconoclast, must defend tradition. She must argue that the artist cut off from tradition, from his culture, is crippled and may react in bizarre, unforeseen ways. He may, like the Anglo-Irish writers Wilde and Shaw, use wit, the characteristic weapon of this group, to attack the system he does not accept and still even be lionized in response. Another kind of disaffiliated artist may wish to celebrate this world but be denied the opportunity to inherit a system he can accept, so he falls back on his own resources. This response can mean the long blank years of Kipling's later life, or the fantastic, personally fabricated philosophy of Yeats, or the excessively refined social constructs of Henry James's assessive sensibility. Rebecca West herself has affinities with this group. She is the child of a Scots mother and an Anglo-Irish father whose ancestors went to Ireland in the reign of Edward VI, but she lives in England. She began her career as a feminist attacking a social order that tried to make of her something she did not want to be, and she spent twenty of her mature years preoccupied with the nature of treason, an extreme form of disassociation. For her to defend tradition here is for her to stress the value of something she has been denied and has attacked and later will come to brood upon.

Here, in this essay, West sees tradition working for her. She, a critic, becomes an arbiter of taste, one who assumes certain standards and applies them to works of art. She helps create and perpetuate a general feeling for excellence in art. In her role as critic she is as necessary to the sustenance of quality in society as the inspectors of restaurants or the accreditors of schools. As one who acts both to create and support art, she sees tradition as a positive force that promotes her ability to so act. This is of greater import than it might otherwise be because, in her mind, it is tied to her persistent idea that art and civilization and the individual who participates in them are all caught up in an uneasy contest between life and death. The continuity of art and civilization evidences the continuity of life. In the vigor of her youth West could affirm that human beings have a natural goodness in them that, if left to work its way, can help them create a life-promoting world, if society will let them do so. In her later writings, where the harsher voice of experience is heard, she becomes more cautious:

This confirms my belief that man does not want to progress past a certain point, that he does not want to commit himself wholly to the side of life, that the real source of his troubles is a suicidal impulse which makes him try to wipe out his breed whenever it has got itself established.[22]

For West, art is evidence that we can hold this suicidal impulse in check if we have the desire and will to do so, but that art still reflects our awareness that we live in a hazardous, intractable environment, and that we have that within us which makes us unwilling to commit ourselves wholly to life. So whatever strengthens that commitment, whether it be love, which offers us an amelioration of life's circumstances, or art, which offers us a means of understanding ourselves and the imperatives of our existence, we should value it for its life-saving grace.

In "The Strange Necessity" West attempts an ambitious, unusual task. She tries to answer an old, baffling question and, in the effort, tries to unite the paradoxes she found in art and life, among them one which many thought to be irresolvable, the conflicting interests of art and science. In her effort she tries to blend the idiom of the artist with the idiom of the scientist so that both the artist and the scientist could understand and relate to each other. She accepts modern civilization as it is and tries, in a limited but important area, to make sense of it.

VIII   *American Literature*

The short essays West chose to reprint in *The Strange Necessity* offer the reader no obvious theme or pattern, but they contain two topics that deserve comment. The first is Rebecca West's view of America and its literature. After her initial trip to the United States in 1923, she came back for frequent, extended visits during which she developed friendships and associations, particularly with Harold Ross and his *New Yorker* friends and contributors. From the 1930s through the 1950s she wrote as often for such American newspapers and periodicals as the *New York Herald Tribune,* the *New Yorker,* and *Harper's* as she did for the *London Daily Telegraph, Time and Tide,* and *Nash's "Pall Mall" Magazine.* She traveled over much of the United States and wrote about what she saw and did, often with greater perception and less British provincialism than usually is exhibited by her compatriots. America of the 1920s and 1930s reached out with naive enthusiasm for things British. Both she and America benefited from the relationship.

Despite the close association, she remains in her writing about America a European. She came to observe and judge, not to accept, not to become at one with it. With Europe's past permeating her thought and weighting her judgment, she endorsed the view expressed by Henry James and others that American society still lacked a tradition which could adequately substitute for what its erstwhile immigrants had discarded, and that American authors suffered from that lack. She carries this point even further and argues that any cultural cohesiveness that could have developed from America's Puritan origins had been adulterated and muddied by recurring waves of immigrants from various cultures. West saw the consequence appearing in exaggerated forms of idiosyncratic behavior, often antisocial, often violent. More at home in the relative intimacy of "this sceptred isle," "this little world" of England, she thought that the hugeness of America, coupled with the monotonous sameness of its heartland, stimulated in Americans a tendency toward introspection that, unchecked and uncriticized by long established heterogeneities of the kind that existed in Europe, made them fix obsessively on a single ideal and intolerantly resist anything that might oppose it. In happier moments she could praise America's optimism and admire its boisterous, freedom-loving qualities. On balance, though, she keeps a cool eye and a sharp tongue.

Her reading of American literature appears extensive but unsystematic; again we observe the consequence, it would seem, of book reviewing. What she presents is like a broken mirror, shining fragments that offer us no complete image, nothing, for example, to compare with D. H. Lawrence's *Studies in Classic American Literature.* The isolated images we do find reflected in these fragments leave us at times shaking our heads until we remember her remark, made when commenting on American reviews of British books, that the best of critics "can miss the significance of a work of art through insufficient knowledge of the civilization which produces it."[23]

To look first at those authors she neglects. Howells bores her. Dreiser fell victim to a brash review she wrote when she was still new at the trade; she drags him forth this once, flaying him for that commonplace, his style, and then pushes him back into obscurity. Faulkner she finds obscure, or indecent, or, even worse, lacking in talent. Hemingway elicits noncommittal comments. Fitzgerald she mentions in passing on to some other, more important topic. Edith Wharton, to her, seemed an anachronism trying to couple a method learned from James with situations too crude to justify it. She has passed over here a distinguished list of authors. Her judgment has not stood the test of time very well.

The well-known American authors she saw fit to include in *The Strange Necessity* are Sinclair Lewis, Sherwood Anderson,

and Willa Cather. To her, Sinclair Lewis was more than a name
and a row of books. He was a personality, a legend. With
uncharacteristic hyperbole she described him in an essay not
included in *The Strange Necessity* as "a flaming figure of
Homeric strength and intensity. . .with the vitality of a god and
the gestures of a rebel, and [yet with] something curious in his
inhabiting spirit which makes the final effect of everything he
says or does grotesquely comic."[24] This has the making of legend,
but the figure is not heroic. West praises Lewis as a satirist,
typical of that older, lean, rural American who differs markedly
from the archetype he, Lewis, created, the heavier, sentimental,
optimistic, urban Babbitt. But Lewis's misfortune, West believed,
was to be a satirist in, of all places, America, that country in
which satire, ordinarily one of the last products of civilization,
has developed prematurely and in excess. As a result, he was
both feared and misunderstood. So when *Babbitt* appeared, the
Babbitts of America knew no better than to join the satirist in
bruising laughter. For the satirist this could mean only frustration
because his ultimate purpose was denied to him. He was
misunderstood.

She finds less to praise in her review of Lewis's *Elmer Gantry,*
the review she included in *The Strange Necessity.* She credits the
author with having a gift for rendering reality that has seldom
been surpassed, but she balances that off against his lapses into
dull writing and flaccid use of events, which add up to formless
books that end because their author "had come to the end of the
writing pad."[25] This is to say that he did not take time to consider
seriously what he wanted to do. As a European she lectures him:
"If he would sit still so that life could make any deep impression
on him, if he would attach himself to the human Tradition by
occasionally reading a book which would set him a standard of
profundity, he would give his genius a chance."[26]

Sherwood Anderson was the only one of that group of
American expatriates living in Paris after World War I to draw
from West any sustained comment, a fact that seems strange
when one recognizes that the interests of these expatriates seem
very close to West's own. She could have found in their work
what she, as critic, thought to be important: a lively interest in
experimentation as well as a commitment to art. Also, they were
in Paris, a city she frequented both when they were there and
later. She bought the copy of James Joyce's poems that activated

her essay "The Strange Necessity" in Sylvia Beach's bookstore, a haunt of these Americans. She wrote both early and late about Ford Madox Ford, who used his position on the *Transatlantic Review* to provide Hemingway and others of the Lost Generation with their first audience. But she leaves these possible alliances unnoted.

Anderson she admired, up to a point. Though he wrote fiction, she saw him as a poet because of his ability to see beauty in anything and to make it vibrant and alive. Like some other writers she has singled out to praise, he was fascinated by psychology. He could be silly at times, she thought, when he was caught up in his emotions, but when he could make that emotion vibrate truly, then he became the American writer of his generation West thought she had most reason to envy.

The writing of Willa Cather, to West a "classic artist," has a quality West admires wherever she finds it: palpability, sensory realism. This can be thought of as just another way for West to say that she celebrates life, and that this manifestation of it suits her very well. She appreciates Cather's willingness to live in the present and to be neither guilt-ridden nor dissatisfied while doing so. To feel that guilt and to aspire for that which is not of the here and now constitutes an opposing mode that West recognizes as resulting in a different kind of art. It is to her the mode of the Puritan, the mode of D. H. Lawrence, a different kind of artist whom she admired just as greatly. She valued the achievement of both and saw them as existing in a symbiosis as natural and meaningful as the rotation of the seasons, with Cather as Ceres and Lawrence following the darker path of Persephone. The miracle left unnoted by West is how Cather, the classic artist, could have flowered and borne fruit in Puritan America.

IX *West's "Uncles"*

The second topic in the short essays deserving comment is West's evaluation of those authors of the previous generation she called her "uncles." There are four of them: Arnold Bennett, John Galsworthy, George Bernard Shaw, and H. G. Wells. For her to call them uncles is to suggest that they had an avuncular literary relation with her, that they influenced her in some special way, and that she remembered them with fondness. But some of this must be said with tongue in cheek; Bennett she considered her implacable foe; Galsworthy she described as evolving too much into a dull-witted, mechanical fellow; Shaw was once her shining hero, a champion of women's rights, but she later found that he could be a silly man as well, especially in his affairs with women; and Wells she knew as a lover with whom the emotional bond was so strong he thought of himself as her husband.

The influence of these uncles would have been felt early, beginning while West was an impressionable young girl. They would have helped determine her developing sense of what the artist was, what his purpose might be. They all display some characteristics of the Edwardian era's impulse to change, to shuck off the old ways which were seen as oppressive to the individual and his happiness. Generally they fought for the underdog, the disadvantaged. They were artists of persuasion and their books were their weapons.

Of the four, Bennett had the least interest in reforming economics and politics, and thus "stood for a purer liberation. He stood for the emancipation of the phenomenon, for the establishment of democracy among the perceptions."[27] West saw him as her Protestant uncle, one whose predilections were to dislike the picturesque and the grand style, to avoid the celebration, the high moment, in favor of the even flow of mundane event. His strength lay there, in his fondness for the commonplace. He used "his power of empathy to enter each of his characters in turn, to imagine how each of them would have reacted to all of their experiences."[28] In his ability to elicit an equivalent empathy from his readers lay his success as a creator of public sympathy and opinion, as a stimulator in that public of an urge to reform.

Galsworthy felt with greater urgency the desire to reform society, so West describes him as her phagocyte uncle, that agent in the blood which rushes to the seat of infection and eats up the hostile bacteria. She found in him, as she did in so many other authors of his generation, an impulse to write of public life as if, in a confused way, he anticipated the millennium. Corruption was everywhere around him; his task was to point it out and exhort the sinners to be cleansed. But West was not sure Galsworthy could always distinguish the pure of heart from the sinner, especially in his Forsyte novels, where his sympathies were most engaged. Too quick to luxuriate in the sentiment of pity and too easily satisfied with the appearance of things, he did not seem to comprehend the full moral import of what he created. West puzzled over this quality in him and how it related to his popularity, but decided finally that the public also thrived on sentimentality and responded to characters that had only the appearance of life. Galsworthy suited them very well, even if he could not satisfy critics like herself.

As West describes him, Uncle Shaw had a mind like a fine French watch, a thin, polished case enclosing intricate, carefully worked machinery which keeps precise time. Reason was his instrument of reform, reason in the guise of wit. Like Voltaire and Gibbon before him, "he popularized the use of the intellectual processes among the politically effective class. And he did it with such style."[29] West's first memory of him was as a missionary for the Fabian Society, preaching a melioristic message of economic reform. He did as much for the feminist movement, and West paid him the supreme compliment that, were it not for his efforts, women in Britain would not have voted and held public office as soon as they did. Yet she saw him as a *thin* watch, which to her meant that there was an inconclusiveness and lack of depth in his thinking, plus a tendency to respond to just the problem of the moment. Still, West values more highly than most the working of a fine intellect, so Shaw was for her an uncle worth emulating, as long as she was not taken in by his shortcomings as well.

Wells was the uncle West most enjoyed. He "arrived always a little out of breath, with his arms full of parcels, sometimes rather carelessly tied, but always bursting with all manner of attractive gifts. . . ."[30] He enjoyed life, but he would have liked it better if everyone else would live it on his terms, so his gifts usually were educational toys that he had invented. Not that he was intolerant, for he enjoyed a good argument, and since by nature he effervesced and let the momentary excitement carry him where it would, he could find himself pushed into what at some other time he would have considered an untenable position. West thrives on argument as much as Wells did; her audacious attack on one of his novels led to their initial meeting. But she soon became possessive of her favorite uncle; she could criticize him, but she did not like anyone else to do so. As much as anyone, he taught her how exciting the world of ideas could be.

He taught her that fiction could be created out of the contest of one of those ideas with another. He reinforced what her real father had already taught her, that politics and science were two human activities that merited her attention.

Elsewhere West has described her relation with the generation of her father as one of hostility. Her "uncles," though, would all have been younger brothers to her father, thus capable of bridging the gap between the generations with more ease than someone nearer her father's age. One does not detect hostility between West and her "uncles," if that relationship is restricted to their literary influence on her. For her the relationship is closer to one of initial admiration tempered later by an awareness of fallibility, of lessons learned and then partially discarded.

X *British Contemporaries*

A reader should not go to Rebecca West's books to find her comments on her contemporary British literary colleagues. She has written about all of them, but she included very little of it in *The Strange Necessity* and *Ending in Earnest,* so if one wants to know what she had to say about Virginia Woolf or Aldous Huxley or E. M. Forster or Ford Madox Ford, one must look among her uncollected essays. When she did include James Joyce in *The Strange Necessity,* it was because he was useful to her in developing a more general, more theoretical topic. For her, thesis tends to prevail over personality, analysis over description.

The closest she comes to accepting the author as justification in himself is in the group of "appreciations" she wrote of authors at their deaths. She began this practice early with her book on Henry James, and continued it with the essays she wrote on Arnold Bennett, Rudyard Kipling, and D. H. Lawrence when they died. Lawrence seems to have affected her most deeply, for she had her eulogy of him reprinted twice after it first appeared. He exemplified so much that was important to her: his celebration of life, his overpowering genius, his willingness to attack taboos. For his attack on the taboo on sex, he met with confiscation and censorship. He could have known of West's defense when his pictures were confiscated by the police from a London gallery, but he did not live to see West, in 1961, do her part to lift the legal ban on his work that most symbolized this effort, *Lady Chatterley's Lover.*

Her most characteristic practice was to use her contemporaries either as case studies or as illustrations for some theory she wished to develop. With either method she subordinated the author to what she saw as the larger interest she wished to develop. If the author becomes a case study, then West deduces her conclusion from the evidence she accumulates, as she does when, in what is probably the best example, though not of a British author, she describes in her essay on Gide[31] how she reread his works in order to arrive at an understanding why she, without previously having thought out why, found him wanting as an author. Each of his books she reads adds its evidence until she concludes that he is an adult manqué, one who, living still in childish fantasies, fails to test those fantasies against the realities of experience. He is a case study in arrested development, an example of that immature impulse in some men to blame women for their failures. Gide's homosexuality made him particularly vulnerable to such a charge, which West, with her dislike for what she would consider as a misuse of the sexual impulse, did not hesitate to point out.

To turn to the second method, the use of an author's work to illustrate a more general theory, we have noted already the best example, her use of Joyce as illustration of facets of her theory that great art consists of analysis and synthesis resulting in an excitatory complex, with the purpose to promote life and to push forward the front edge of the culture. Of all her British contemporaries, she selected two as best fitting the criteria of that theory, Virginia Woolf and Aldous Huxley.

Virginia Woolf exemplified for West both a perceptive intelligence superbly equipped for the artist's process of analysis and synthesis, and an original mind capable of creating new fictive constructs. Refuting accusations of snobbery directed at Woolf and the Bloomsbury Group to which she belonged, West insisted that Woolf observed life acutely, accurately, taking in at a glance what required others more than a long stare to half understand. She was superior, not a snob. In making this judgment, West relies on Woolf's writing rather than an intimate acquaintance as her source because neither West nor anyone of the Bloomsbury Group have left any evidence that they associated closely. Woolf's vision was attuned to the fine psychological nuances of human action that became so large a part of her fiction. In West's opinion, Woolf was that artist of her generation most apt to survive. Significant as this judgment would otherwise be, it is made more so by Woolf's being a woman because West, who shows a special sensitivity for the problems a creative woman faces, would have scrutinized her work carefully both for evidence of general excellence and for the absence of that feminine self-consciousness she had found too often in her reading of other female artists.

West includes Aldous Huxley in the select group primarily because he is a thinker, an artist who, like H. G. Wells, was knowledgeable of modern thought, particularly science, and could project its implications into the future. When she reviewed *Brave New World* she was interested primarily in the social pattern he constructed. She saw its relevance, both in its similarity to what the Behaviorists were then advocating and in its restatement of the old theme of man's unwillingness to accept Christ, modernized here by Huxley's use of twentieth-century science's capacity to control thought and, for the purposes of efficiency, to dehumanize the political process. The mature Huxley appealed to that part of Rebecca West's critical perception that valued incisive thought and enjoyed the exercise of moving back and forth between idea and object, a process in which the object is not so much symbol as it is instrument and the idea is valued not so much for its quality as for its effectiveness. Huxley, unlike Lawrence, does not emerge in West's critique of him as a sentient, vibrant person whose imagination is his glory and curse. He appears, rather, as a mind, an intelligence, given to enough variance in the quality of what it creates to show that it is, after all, a human intelligence.

XI   Ending in Earnest

Ending in Earnest is not so significant a book as *The Strange Necessity*, but it is more readable. The essays Rebecca West collected in it are all drawn from the series "Letters from Europe" she prepared for the *Bookman*. In her foreword to the book West states that the personal quality of the letters should not be looked on "as a sign of undue egotism on my part, but as a result of the agreement between myself and the editor that this was the most useful form they could take at the time; and their episodic nature is due to that cause also."[32] Varied, uneven, impressionistic, informal, these letters combine travel sketch with aesthetic and historic comment. They are on whatever topics catch West's attention as she moves about Europe: Max Beerbohm's unease in a gathering of women authors, West in a villa in the south of France, her meditating on death in a church at Tournus, her glimpsing Virginia Woolf and Colette. Even her eulogy to D. H. Lawrence is included. Here West seems to be at ease with the form. Though probably she did not foresee its further usefulness, her success with it in these letters serves as an apprenticeship to her use of it later in the occasional "Notes on the Way" she published in *Time and Tide* and in her two-volume study of Yugoslavia, *Black Lamb and Grey Falcon*.

As a title, *Ending in Earnest* does not appear to have as direct an application to the book's contents as *The Strange Necessity* does to the topic of that book. *Ending in Earnest* suggests some other purpose for which the book serves as symbol. It can be read as West's declaration of the end of that phase in her career which had as its central concern the definition and purpose of art. She seems to have come to this conclusion with some difficulty, else the term *earnest* would not have been needed. But if one reads it in the context of her shift of attention from art to politics because of what she saw as the growing threat of totalitarianism in Europe, as well as the conclusion she set to her relation with H. G. Wells by her impending marriage to Henry Maxwell Andrews, then she is indeed ending this phase of her life in earnest.

If one prefers not to look so autobiographically at the title, then one can justify it by its relation to the book's final essay, entitled here "Regretfully," which had on its first appearance in the *Bookman* the title "A Last Letter. A counterblast to humanism." With this essay West put an end to a debate she had engaged in with the American advocates of New Humanism. Six months earlier she had published in the *New York Herald Tribune* an essay, "The Benda Mask," in which her main target was T. S. Eliot, but her shot was scattered widely enough to include others who held his views. T. S. Eliot she had known since they were young editors on the *Egoist* during World War I, and she had disapproved of him in print on more than one occasion. So, as far as Eliot was concerned, West repeated in

"The Benda Mask" what she had said already. The new element was her enlarging her criticism to include Americans like Paul Elmer More and Irving Babbitt, identified with the New Humanist movement, and a group of French neoclassic writers represented for her by Benda, Maurras, and Maritain. Her singling out of Benda, whose best-known book, *La Trahison des Clercs,* is an attack on modern intellectuals as betrayers of their own kind, for a prominent identification in her title has the additional effect of forcing the debate out of its literary context and into politics.

West's criticism of Eliot includes the following: he impressed her as sententious, paralyzed by his desire to be distinguished and authoritative, driven by an impulse to escape reality, prone to reiterating formulae, and apt to display an intellectual confusion when making pronouncements about matters he had not studied carefully enough. These are serious accusations. West did not direct them at Eliot the poet, for his achievement there she considered true and splendid. Rather, they were directed at Eliot the critic, the writer of essays, where both his beliefs and his attributes as a student of the past would be more obvious. She was critical of his language which seemed to her more appropriate for one engaged in a laying on of hands than for one assuming the more conventional critical posture of doing battle. Ridiculing his tendency to stand in awe of traditional institutions that seem less haloed to those who have lived with them from birth, she stigmatized him as a leader of what she termed the "call to order" critics who looked at the chaos of the modern world with dismay and presumed they had all the weight of tradition supporting their pronouncements.

Much of West's criticism of Eliot applies as well to the New Humanists. They too were given to sententious pronouncements, to preaching conformist doctrine, to bemoaning the present and cherishing the past. When the New Humanists were in the midst of their controversy with the Naturalists in the early 1930s, West was serving as an editor with Wells, Huxley, and others on the *Realist,* a British journal advocating scientific humanism, an approach which suggests a similar emphasis on being human, but indicates in its championing of science a different orientation than the conservative, religious humanism of Babbitt and More. She also was busy with her series for the *New York Herald Tribune* and for the *Bookman.* Both served her as forums for her argument, which reached its climax in her last contribution to the *Bookman* (August 1930), the same essay she placed at the conclusion of *Ending in Earnest,* in which she explained why she had "to go." In this essay she reiterated her revulsion at the self-righteousness of the New Humanists and objected to the stultifying influence they would have on young artists who, subscribing to this easy, accessible "faith," would soon find themselves on the way to sterile complacency. Unwilling to accept the either-or premise of their doctrine, West argued that the New Humanists were wrong-headed in promoting their thesis that the romantic-classic duality was an antagonistic relationship. To her that relationship was a continuous, integrated process. The process begins when the artist finds new material. He gives himself to it intellectually and emotionally, and then expresses his reaction. What he has done is unsettling to him and to others. He has broken

the mould of the universe as it was before this new experience was added to it. Then he is romantic. If he remakes the mould of the universe, incorporating the new experience and reestablishing the order which he had previously undone, he is a classicist. . . . It is therefore no use denouncing the romantic. He is a necessary precursor of the classic.[33]

So where the New Humanists saw a pernicious attitude that must be eradicated, she saw only a natural and all-welcome process of art.

Insofar as the New Humanists accepted Benda and his arguments, she would have rejected them as well. His "offensive sugar style"[34] put her off at the start. His view that the intellectual became a traitor to his fellow intellectuals when he accepted his responsibilities as a citizen, when he used his knowledge for public service, when he valued something closer to the whole experience over pure reason, just as quickly would have set her teeth on edge, if for no reason other than that her own feminist convictions assured her that the opposite was true. If her own convictions would not have been enough, then she needed to look no further than H. G. Wells, who had committed his life and talent to his political realization of One World. Benda added a political dimension to the dispute that she could not ignore. Benda and Babbitt and More and, in his way, Eliot were, in effect, attacking some of West's most abiding commitments, her justification for being. They were also helping create that malaise of spirit that she saw spreading over Europe. She could not keep quiet, nor could she remain in any consenting relation, however tacit, with them. She had "to go."

XII   Waugh's Libel Action

West's conviction that art and politics are intimately interrelated came to public notice again even more dramatically in 1956, twenty-five years later. In the revision of *The Meaning of Treason* she prepared for the paperback Pan edition, she added a passage in which she described the effect certain novelists had had on the society in which the traitors she presented in her book had developed. After commenting that the spirit of the age required people to condemn the traitor, but still encouraged them to find in him a style, an elegance, a subtlety that to them was attractive, she continued: "The bases of this peculiar judgment are not often stated openly in journalism, which is the field in which treason is most often discussed, and the best way to discover them is by an indirect approach through the imaginative literature of our time."[35] From this comment she passed to the fiction of Graham Greene and Evelyn Waugh, where she found characteristics she thought contributed to the glamorization of the traitor. Instead of merely saying that the literature was symptomatic of the social ethos, she suggested that they, the authors, had created this intellectual climate and the social misanthropy that it generated. The statement had enough of a direct consignment of moral blame in it to cause Evelyn Waugh, already disturbed by an attack on him in the *Daily Express,* to bring a libel action, which was settled in his favor, with the book being withdrawn from the market and the defendants, the publisher and the printer, indemnifying him for costs.[36] Rebecca West did not take part in the action. The incident poses the paradox that if West had made her judgment on aesthetic principles, which she as a literary critic had done with equal sharpness many times before, the author criticized might not have liked what she wrote, but he would more likely have stopped short of legal recourse. But in *The Meaning of Treason* West, writing as a journalist, is making social and moral judgments, so Evelyn Waugh did find there reason enough to seek legal relief. The episode suggests that West felt even more strongly in 1956 than she did in 1931 that society not only deserves the literature it fosters but that it must pay the consequences as well. In 1931 she "ended in earnest" her literary criticism to turn to what she thought were more significant political and social changes. By 1956, after witnessing the effects of a depression and its stimulation of a social consciousness in literature, plus a world war and its frantic manipulation of the word for political purposes, she judges literature, at least in this example, more as an instrument than as an achievenemt containing its own justification, and, if skillfully used, it may become a weapon powerful enough to effect an erosion of social values. Her argument becomes more intense, but it remains consistent; neither Benda's intellectual nor West's artist can consider himself unaccountable to society. Through both incidents runs the sinister theme of treason.

XIII   The Court and the Castle

A later, more impressive example of West's preoccupation with the social significance of literature is her book *The Court and the Castle,* her reworking of the Terry Lectures she presented at Yale in 1957. In this book her basic interest is to examine the nature of the individual, the courtier as she calls him, and his historically shifting relationship to his society, the court, both of them affected by his intent to enter the castle of God. Literature here is not conceived as propaganda or as an instrument for winning arguments. Nor is it even so much explanation as it is something more worthwhile, the artistic bodying forth of reflection. For the suggestion of her theme, West quotes from Paul Valéry:

"It must be remembered that our greatest authors have nearly always written only about the court. They drew on the life of the city only for comedy, and on the country for fables. But the greatest art, the art of integrated form and pure types of character. . .is bound up with the existence of a society governed by convention, where a language is spoken that is adorned with veils and furnished with limits, where *to seem* controls *to be* and holds it nobly in a constraint which changes the whole of life into an exercise in the control of the mind."[37]

Her purpose in the book is to trace the shifting interrelationship of court and courtier from Shakespeare to Kafka. She began with Shakespeare because for him the court was a specific, identifiable place and the courtiers were few enough that they could be set apart and characterized. The question West finds of nagging concern to Shakespeare, the question that determined the relation of the courtier to the court, was the source from which the king, the fulcrum on which the court turned, derived his power. Whatever that source—divine right, rightful inheritance, military force, popularity—to Shakespeare it seemed unstable, as if set in shifting sand. But how could the king be otherwise, since his court and courtiers too were imperfect? Court and courtiers would appear to have a community of interest, if it were only mutual survival. The courtier did need the court, but the court could find it in its interest to turn on the courtier and destroy him. The courtier might try to sweeten his imperfection, as Hamlet did, by what he thought to be a righteous deed, but the deed itself is flawed. Despite the historical moment of exceptional splendor in which he lived, Shakespeare found in no element of the court an evidence of benign purpose in the universe. Hamlet dies, Richard II is murdered, Othello is betrayed by Iago, and their queens and ladies are but queens and ladies in jest, used to fill a scene and then be abandoned to mourn their dead loved ones.

West picks up her theme again in the eighteenth century of Henry Fielding. Though in the court he describes the customs of society had brushed a veneer of civilization over the fierce splendors of the Renaissance, he still found wickedness there. But his court had been enlarged; the courtiers were more numerous, so that wickedness was diffused. It was more venal perhaps, but less murderous. Old fierce distinctions of class no longer held, so evil could show the same face in the fine mansions of London as it did in Newgate prison. Yet Fielding still was a meliorist; his courtiers cared for liberty and fraternity and his court contained ladies who functioned not so much as instruments of state policy as agents of redemptory grace.

From Fielding West moved to Jane Austen, whose court is the country house and whose ceremony is high tea or the cotillion. The courtiers still jostle for position, but the game is marriage and the contestants are often as not the ladies of the court. The number of courtiers has grown larger, though the positions into which they can fit have not. Inevitably some fail, but their fate is to be tolerated, not to meet a violent death. Though her preference was for the court, Austen's interest was in the individual courtier, even if she smiled and thought his condition ridiculous. She recognized that his immortal soul existed and she did not present his will as corrupt, yet she still portrayed him as accepting compromise as the way to moral virtue. The ladies of Jane Austen's court did not redeem it; they assured its decorum and continuity.

Austen's preference for the court West saw continued by Scott, Thackeray, Dickens, and Trollope, each in his own way stressing the representativeness of the individual, his aptness to conform to the group or institution of which he was a part. The blaze of ego of the Renaissance courtier has dwindled into class and professional mannerisms. To the degree that the human will was capable of order, it functioned best when asserted through the group. The increase in the number of courtiers had intensified even more their contesting for appropriate positions. But even this growing strain put on the court did not, in the minds of these authors, jeopardize its value. It still gave shelter to the courtiers and helped save them from damnation. The ladies of their court could still function as redeemers, but with greater frequency they abandoned their special status and, for the sake of self-interest, elbowed their way into the crowd.

The revolutionary spirit of the end of the eighteenth century that had passed Austen by and had left the basic preference of her successors intact, broke through in Hardy and Meredith. They reversed the preference of their predecessors, favoring the courtier to the court, though their quarrel with the court was temporary because they saw it as flawed but capable of being perfected. This they partially could do by adding to Fielding's liberty and fraternity the still missing element in the revolutionary triad, equality.

To this point the development that West has traced seems continuous. With James and Conrad she found an interruption. They seemed to her to reach back to earlier assumptions. They expected the court to carry the burden of moral significance that Shakespeare had assumed it did. They saw it as a model in miniature for achieving salvation or damnation. But they misread the model. James put too much stress on ceremony and Conrad saw his courtier as so weak that the court was in constant danger of being nullified by his weakness. Despite the evidence they could observe of society's unmanageable growth, both James and

Conrad arbitrarily limited the number of courtiers they permitted in their courts. James still expected the lady to carry the moral burden. Conrad excluded her. As commentators on the social evolution they were witnessing, each in his way is urging us to keep in mind what he sees as the traditional moral obligation of the courtier. Each prefaces his statement with the caution: "Lest we forget."

For the rest of her description of this historical process, West turned to Continental authors. As one of them she chose Proust because he described the dissolution of the court as the conclusion to the process she was describing. In part, sheer numbers had caused this dissolution, but an equally effective cause was capitalist democracy with its jostling, unresponsive segments of self-interest. Proust described a society in which if something went amiss, everyone and no one could be blamed. "The court, which so many writers had conceived as an entity in its own right, benevolently assisting the courtier to check the corruption of their individual wills, was no help to Proust or to his characters."[38] It was no help because it was no longer identifiable. The courtiers are left in chaos to shift for themselves.

West's other choice was Kafka because he described the other possible conclusion, the metamorphosis of the court into a faceless, all-powerful bureaucracy. Kafka differed from Shakespeare in his unwillingness to accept impurity. The true bureaucrat assumes that perfection is attainable. He assumes also the necessity of strict obedience to the rules of the bureaucracy. It is not surprising, then, that Kafka believed the will of man to be more foully corrupt than did Shakespeare. To will requires that one know what one is willing for or against, but Kafka's world denies that knowledge to the individual caught in the bureaucratic maze. Still, Kafka thought more highly of the court than did Shakespeare. Kafka leaves us with the impression that the courtier, who once was particularized, important, has dwindled into a barely significant pawn, a factor for bureaucratic manipulation. His relation to the court is a diminished agony.

The pattern Rebecca West traces in *The Court and the Castle* has as its central motivation humanity's desire for salvation. Perceptions of how, or if, this salvation could be attained differed as the authors she chose swung between two opposing concepts of man's nature: the orthodox doctrine of man's innate evil versus the Pelagian heresy of man's perfect free will. The adherence of these authors to one or the other of these opposing concepts determined as well whether they favored the court or the courtier. West's pattern began historically with the graphic particularity of a limited number of courtiers in a specific Renaissance court and ended in the amorphous grayness of impersonal forces that characterizes modern society. As West describes it, this relation of court to courtier has been basically a masculine interest, but running through it is a feminist concern that points to the horrors that women suffered as instruments of political policy in the Renaissance court, to their serving as agents of the male's redemption in the eighteenth and nineteenth centuries, and finally to their fading back into the nondistinguishing blur of the twentieth century.

The Court and the Castle is testimony to West's conviction that literature of a high order most often has as its topic man's effort to develop a political order that will enhance his existence in this life and promote his search for the divine. In her examination of this literature she has gone her own way, searching for what she thinks of value there and seeking no alliance with what critics may accept as currently orthodox. Her ability to sustain her argument as she passes through large masses of material and long periods of time is a remarkable demonstration of memory and inventive organization. Early in her career she won Frank Swinnerton's praise for producing what became the representative fragments from which this book is constructed. Through all of the subsequent years West held true to her conviction that the individual's well being could not be separated from the social matrix in which he exists. She was committed to the courtier and hoped to change the court. Her hope of something better could not have envisioned what she has lived to see that courtier and court become, but the hope has moderated to cautious wisdom, and rebellious impatience to a measure of acceptance.

CHAPTER 3

Journalist and Historian

I Early Journalism

REBECCA West was never a reporter in the conventional sense; she made no daily rounds of the railroad station, the hospital, and the police station as Ernest Hemingway did when he worked for the *Kansas City Star.* The closest she came to being that kind of a journalist was when she worked for the *Clarion,* but there, even though she did describe the efforts of the women to secure the right to vote, she did so as an advocate of women's suffrage in articles that are half editorial, half feature story, rather than regular news reports. The humdrum aspect of her professional journalistic life, then and later, was given to reading and writing about books. Her excursions into contemporary political and social events appear as moments of release from that routine.

Aside from her work for the *Clarion,* those moments are few and far between in the first twelve years of her career, and even then the subjects she wrote on were still either literature or feminism. The opportunity came to her from America. A new venture in journalism, whose editor stated its purpose to be "less to inform or entertain its readers than to start little insurrections in the realm of their convictions,"[1] appeared on November 7, 1914. This journal was the *New Republic.* An essay by Rebecca West appears in its first issue, so she and this distinguished journal began their American careers together.

Her essay, her effort to start a little insurrection in the minds of her readers, had the title "Duty of Harsh Criticism." In it she ridiculed her British colleagues for vitiating their usefulness as reviewers with their bland, noncommittal politeness. They should be replaced, she wrote, by "a new and abusive school of criticism."[2] Her essay has the tone of a manifesto, though what she was advocating here she had been practicing since her *Freewoman* days, and with more finesse she would still use it half a dozen years later as the informing dictum of her "Notes on Novels" series, which Swinnerton praised.

She followed this declaration of purpose with four other articles in the *New Republic,* all on literary topics appearing at monthly intervals. In one of them she attacked the "eroto-priggery"[3] of Ellen Key, a writer then generally accepted as a public duenna attending to women's behavior. In another she mixed politics and literature, arguing unconvincingly that Britain found it easier to accept Russia as a wartime ally because the British public had read and liked Russian fiction. Though she may have seemed a new, spirited voice to the American reader, in none of these essays does she attempt anything distinctively different from what she had been offering British readers.

About one year later, beginning in January 1916, she published in the *New Republic* five more essays, this time on the topic "woman: the world's worst failure." Drawing on what she had seen and experienced in wartime England, she moved from one category of women to another, describing how in each instance they perpetuated attitudes that were self-defeating. Whether she was the factory worker who acquiesced in her own exploitation, or the school mistress who helped neuter her own femininity, or the lady who had made a fine art of her artificiality just for the purpose of loving and being loved, they all clung to some concept of elegance as a feminine attribute they desired. Even those who seemed most unlikely and who could least afford it fell victim with all the others.

These five essays differ from the previous series in their perception, their probing for meaning, particularly when their author describes some personal experience. At times she acknowledges these experiences as her own, like the glimpse she gives us of her school days at what we may presume to be George Watson's Ladies' College, where she was so unhappy she escaped as soon as she could. Other experiences that could have been hers she hides behind a less specific identification, as when she recounts the daily life of an unnamed lady with a small child, who, moving from one place to another and left increasingly to fend for herself in wartime Britain, finds the problems of making do increasingly difficult. The feminist topics West presents here she had addressed before, and the quality of her presentation fluctuates, but the reader still can find here enough evidence of that quickness of eye and thought and that adroitness of phrase to anticipate the celebrated journalist to come.

In October of the following year, 1917, West published two more reports describing the condition of women in wartime Britain. They are factual, researched reports that lack the personal element of the previous series. The first report describes the unsatisfactory conditions and the exploitation of the women in the munitions factories. The second report explores the government's inadequate effort to monitor and correct these conditions. These two reports bring to an end a spurt of reporting on British women in wartime.

II *Trip to America*

In 1923 Rebecca West made her first trip to the United States. This trip opened new possibilities for her as a journalist. Not only did she see a new world and alter old relationships, she lectured, met new people, formed new ideas, saw new modes of behavior. But perhaps just as important, she tried to put her impressions and excitement into new forms of writing; she became a traveling correspondent. For the *New Republic* she wrote her impressions of America, and when she returned to England she crossed to the Continent and described her impressions, still for the *New Republic,* of the effects the Versailles Treaty had had on Austria and Hungary. Here she first makes use of the train compartment, a setting the contemporary imagination associated with intrigue and adventure, as a center of her activities. She would use it again, as she did for the beginning of her journey into Yugoslavia in *Black Lamb and Grey Falcon* and, much later, for the climax of her late novel *The Birds Fall Down.*

Between 1924 and 1928 West's efforts at journalism on nonliterary topics were limited mostly to feminist topics. Her name appeared over captions like "Divorce" and "I Regard Marriage with Fear and Horror." West also was well enough accepted by editors and fellow writers to begin to be asked to contribute to books on general topics, as she did in 1925, when she added her essay to those of Bennett, Walpole, Conan Doyle, and others in a volume entitled *My Religion.*

III   Lions and Lambs

Nothing, however, of distinctive importance appeared until 1928, when she collaborated with David Low, the British caricaturist, in a series of sketches, visual and verbal, on well-known personalities of the day. They entitled their joint effort *Lions and Lambs*. In this book Rebecca West chose to identify herself only by the pseudonym "Lynx," probably suggested to her by the petnames "Panther" and "Jaguar" she and Wells used in their personal relationship. Recognizing also her sometimes playfulness with words, one can recognize in the string of terms *lion, lamb, Low,* and *lynx* that playfulness at work.

Lions and Lambs consists of thirty-six sketches by Low, each accompanied by what the book designates as an impressionistic "interpretation" by West, which often has at its center some detail picked up from Low's caricature. David Low's sketches distort reality only with light humor; Rebecca West's comments do the same. If there is a difference, it is that Low's sketches can be enjoyed by anyone. West's comments spring from topical information that makes them less accessible to the general reader.

The people included in the book form a heterogeneous group, but they have one characteristic in common: they were known to the public. They range from the Prince of Wales to George Bernard Shaw, from the Lord Chief Justice to Augustus John. Most of them are either authors or politicians. Some of West's favorites are here: Wells, Galsworthy, Shaw; others, like the physicist Sir William Orpen, she hardly knows at all. No general theme runs through her sketches, unless it is her bemused attitude toward the quirks in the British character.

Her comments tend to be epigrammatic: "One commonly does not hear quite so much about the superiority complex. But it exists";[4] "It is a thankless task to be the perfect embodiment of a transition period."[5] Some of her comments apply as well to her as they do to her subject. In her sketch of the journalist J. L. Garvin she distinguished between publishers and journalists by observing that while publishers love money and power, "a good journalist must love nothing but life."[6] Reminded of her Scots background by Ramsay Macdonald, she noted that "the Scottish Presbyterian tradition . . . though doubtfully effective in

helping men to become saints in heaven certainly keeps them
from making fools of themselves on earth."[7] And finally, never
one to turn her back on a feminist topic, she found her
opportunity in the novelist Clemence Dane.

She is, past all possibility of cure, a woman novelist. Which is to say that
she has not allowed herself to be merely a mirror in which to reflect
life; before treating her material she has treated herself. She has
created herself in the form in which the man-governed modern world,
so far as it can be ascertained from its art, thinks woman ought to be
created. In other words, she moulds herself in the likeness of the
heroine of standard fiction.[8]

Since West too has written novels, the reader is tempted to test
her fiction by the same criteria.

Lions and Lambs is worth looking at just for the glimpses it
gives us of Rebecca West at work doing what she enjoys doing,
discussing people. In his way, Low is discussing people as well.
The prominence of their subjects forces them to touch their
satire in lightly, but they both are deft, and the combined
creation makes a pleasing, amusing harmony.

IV   The Modern "Rake's Progress"

Rebecca West comes closer to catching the spirit of the age in
another collaborative effort she did with David Low, *The
Modern "Rake's Progress"* (1934). Following the model that
Hogarth, the eighteenth-century British artist, used in the series
of sketches he entitled "The Rake's Progress," Low and West
began with the rake inheriting a fortune, followed him through
his various self-indulgences, and returned him to poverty. They
departed from Hogarth, though, in four important particulars:
their rake is basically foolish, not profligate; he marries for social
status, not for money; he loses his fortune not by gambling, but
by falling victim to the machinations of world trade; and he is
seen last in the dole line, not in Bedlam. Hogarth aims his satire
at individual moral depravity. If David Low's pictures alone
were available, one could come to a similar conclusion about the
modern rake. But West's text shifts the burden of moral
depravity onto society. The modern rake is a fool; society
corrupts him by catering to his desires and toadying to his self-
esteem. But whether he is corrupted or not is irrelevant; if he

were as ascetic as a saint the stock market would have insured that he make his final progress in the dole line. West's satire cuts both ways; it satirizes the individual while it condemns a society that has turned the old, reliable values topsy-turvy. For the most part her satire is direct and unadorned. It reads best when she is pursuing her own ideas, not simply explicating Low's pictures.

V The 1930s

The shift of West's interest away from fiction toward biography and modern history apparent in these two books can be seen as well in the series of book reviews she began writing in 1932 for the *Daily Telegraph*. These reviews contained anywhere from two to nine books, sometimes without one novel among them. Most often the books were biographies, and sometimes histories. In January 1934 the series ended. From then until the beginning of World War II West spent much time writing her own fiction. She also prepared commissioned items and wrote some special reports on current topics.

Her commissioned items include the essays "Mrs. Pankhurst" in *The Post Victorians* (1933) and "Elizabeth Montague" in Bonamy Dobree's *From Anne to Victoria* (1937). She contributed a different kind of essay, "The Necessity and Grandeur of the International Ideal," to *Challenge to Death* (1935), a book Storm Jameson prepared in belated reaction to Julien Benda's *La Trahison des Clercs*. Six years earlier West had attacked Benda's views shortly after his book appeared. In this essay she argues in a more moderate tone for the goal H. G. Wells had championed, the establishment of an international order capable of holding in check the excesses of nationalism.

In 1935 West also prepared for *Time and Tide* a series of four reports on the American political scene which she captioned "The New Deal." She went to Washington, where she found the Roosevelt administration sunk in doldrums after its initial flair of energy and success. Shortly before she arrived the Supreme Court had declared the National Recovery Administration Act unconstitutional, and other New Deal efforts she found in confusion. A part of this failure West attributed to Roosevelt. She recognized his attractiveness as a leader, but faulted his organizational ability. Though she found more to criticize in him than most Americans would, she saw no alternative in the

Republican party. All of this makes gloomy, if enlightening, reading, but West animates the latter part of her series with sketches of Roosevelt, Father Coughlin, and most effectively, Huey Long. In the early part of this series she is impressive in her ability to marshal facts in orderly argument, but her quick, intuitive grasp of the particular human phenomenon she is observing in the sections that follow is even more impressive, for she makes Huey Long spring to life before us. Her sense of public drama, which led her later to the courtrooms in which British traitors heard their fates spelled out for them, led her here to similar public settings. She observed Roosevelt in a news conference, Father Coughlin speaking at Madison Square Garden, and Huey Long, whom she had asked to speak to in the senators' visiting room, playing up to her and finding that she too had a quick retort when she needed it, as they stood together talking just before he was to speak in the Senate. There he soon would throw his challenge to the federal government, "including the old bird in the White House,"[9] as to its right to control the spending of federal money in his political fiefdom. The portrait she paints of him still pulses with the feral energy of the man.

In the spring of the following year (1936), Rebecca West made her first visit to Yugoslavia on a lecture tour that took her to various cities and universities. This experience initiated her interest in Yugoslavia which culminated in her book *Black Lamb and Grey Falcon* (1941) and then continued in the form of her work with the BBC during World War II in support of the Yugoslavian guerrilla effort led by Mihailovitch.

VI   *Post-World War II*

After the war the *New Yorker* commissioned her to report a series of trials, beginning in 1945 with the trial of William Joyce, or Lord Haw Haw, as he is better known, continuing through the Nuremberg trials, then a trial for lynching in Greenville, South Carolina, and concluding with a murder trial back in London in 1950. These reports, collected in *The Meaning of Treason* (1947) and *A Train of Powder* (1955), comprise some of the best of Rebecca West's journalism. They demonstrate her mastery of a form which combines her report of the event (here the formal, controlled drama of the trial, wrapped in its layers of history and tradition) with her portrait in depth of the defendant, the individual at the center of the event. Looking back, we can trace the preparation West has undergone to master this form: the literary portraits she wrote in the late 1920s for the *New York Herald Tribune,* the reports she wrote as a correspondent for the *New Republic* which she then modified into the impressionistic, "on-the-go" sketches she wrote for the *Bookman* and *Time and Tide.* As a literary form, all this preparation culminates here in these accounts of historical events that often read with the vividness of fiction, yet carry with amazing ease the burden of fact out of which they are created. West anticipates here that growing interest among contemporary authors in making fact as fascinating as fiction, an interest we can find embodied in such books as Truman Capote's *In Cold Blood* or Norman Mailer's *The Executioner's Song.*

It is anticlimactic to move to West's report of the American political campaign of 1948 published in the *New York Herald Tribune,* or her reports on British problems and German efforts at recovery in the *London Evening Standard* in 1948–49, or her view of McCarthyism published in 1953, first in the London *Sunday Times* and then reprinted in *U.S. News & World Report.* Even West's last large effort as a correspondent, the series she prepared for the London *Sunday Times* in 1960 on the effects of apartheid in South Africa, lack the dramatic perspicacity of her best journalism. She spent three months early in that year traveling in South Africa in preparation for this series of four articles she captioned "In the Cauldron of Africa." The material for drama was there, but even though she reacted strongly to what she saw and heard, she found no one to place at the center of the drama. She did find injustices, cruelties, personal tragedies, which she could describe and explain and grow indignant about, but they remain illustrations that for her never come to a focus as, for example, Nazi Germany does as she presents its last agonies in her reports of the Nuremberg trials.

Rebecca West's reputation as a journalist is high. General allusions to her that appear in print most often identify her by this term "journalist." Some may be thinking of her book reviews or more generally of her reports on the art and literary scene, but others have in mind her reports of post–World War II events in the *New Yorker,* her absorbing description of Yugoslavia, her explanations to her fellow Britains of the strange goings-on in some of their erstwhile colonies. Like many good journalists, she can present the event she is reporting clearly and comprehensively. Like only a few of them, she can, when the occasion is right, make that event and the individuals who participate in it vivid and dramatic. One in a very select group, she can inform that event with its significance as history and as manifestation of the perversity and glory of humanity.

VII *Perception of History*

The desire West expressed early in life to know everything could not be satisfied entirely by rushing about as a journalist studying the contemporary scene. This was one means of gaining that knowledge, but only one. She found other sources as well. One of them was history. She thought of history as a complex of present and past that made a larger whole. She could keep her equilibrium, she felt, only if she had one foot in the present and the other swung far into the past to give her balance. Increasingly from the 1930s on she reveals in the lists of books she read and in her own writing a preoccupation with the record of that past. At first she wanted answers to why her world, Europe, was sliding into the maelstrom of World War II.[10] Somewhere in the collective memory of Western man she thought she might find her answers. For her these answers would mean clarification, knowledge, even wisdom, but not necessarily power. She had listened for years to H. G. Wells's optimistic assumptions that he could, by persuasion, transform his knowledge into a different world order, but she held no such illusions that what she would learn could energize such change, or even induce her own native country, Britain, to draw back from disaster. Her mood in this period more often reflects despair and exasperation than it does hope.

West finds few constants in history. Mostly it is change, flux, movement from present dissatisfactions into what are too often future unpredictabilities. She will have none of Spengler's theory that civilizations grow and decay like biological organisms; it was to her "such poor stuff that it degrades the intellectual life of its time by every instant that it is tolerated."[11] The determinism in the theory offends her, as does Spengler's self-serving use of that same theory to aggrandize his own ego. Some other cyclical or alternating theory of history might appeal to her since she had championed, in her dispute with the New Humanists, the theory that art fluctuated back and forth between the romantic and classic states. When she did encounter a similar view of history in Arthur Koestler's *The Yogi and the Commissar,* she was fascinated by his perception of history as swinging between the yogi who believed in change from within and the commissar who saw change as effected from without. She notes that to Koestler both extremes seem tragic, and the swing between them is the cause for the blood and tears of history. " 'One slope leads to the Inquisition and the Purges; the other to passive submission, to bayoneting and raping.' "[12] She agrees with him that the corrective would be to stop the pendulum swing. But he knows of no way to do it, nor can she recommend any better means, except some vague and vast democratic inertia: "the cure for the pain of history lies elsewhere, in spheres cultivated by millions who were not Commissars or Yogis, who would have got on well enough if the boat had not been rocked."[13] The pendulum theory too often means excess. It means a frequent departure from reason and the golden mean. She cannot accept it.

What she does accept tends to have its origins in other of her concepts of human psychology. History can be seen as cause and reaction, of trial and rectification.

We are all apt to assume that what is to us the *status quo,* the social dispensation under which we were brought up, was fixed purely arbitrarily, and was not the result of experiment, and if there are unsatisfactory elements in this *status quo* we turn back to the antecedent, eagerly recognize its good points, and propose to remove our discomforts by restoring it. Now, that is fundamentally unsound. The antecedent *status* was an experiment which failed, that was why the dispensation we live under now was invented.[14]

The present is predicated on the past, but there is no nice symmetry, no clear alternation of spirit, no discernible cycle, except insofar as the present is a response to a previous experiment that failed, and that it in turn is an experiment that will also fail.

One could still assume, though, that change is effected by dispassionate reason evaluating reality. West is not that sanguine. In her view neither those who make history nor those who record it can achieve that kind of scientific objectivity.

It is amazing to see how history, which one would think had a very good

chance of achieving a purely objective account of events in the external
world, is in fact intensely subjective; and is but another medium which
man uses not to ascertain the nature of reality but to tell himself myths
confirming his primitive prejudices.[15]

We are brought back here to human psychology. Man makes
history in obedience to his nature, he comprehends it by the
same means. The constants of human nature become the
constants of history.

West made the comments quoted above while passing on to
some other topic. Usually she did not expand on them. However,
let her get started on some specific historical topic and she seems
swept away by the rush of fact and comment the topic excites in
her. So it was in a London nursing-home when she told the nurse
about the Empress Elizabeth of Austria. The nurse had heard
that the Empress was beautiful and that she was mad. Rebecca
West agreed to her beauty but demurred about the madness,
emphasizing instead her cleverness and political statesmanship.
Then caught up in her subject, West recited the details of
Elizabeth's history until, seeing that the nurse was bored, she let
her leave. In part this is so because history is people. Let West
comment on the Jameson Raid and she inevitably thinks of her
uncle, who was made the tragic scapegoat of that misadventure.
Leave her in a memorable church and she tells us of those who
are buried there or who helped make it what it is. Let her open a
book on the French Revolution and she catches us up with her in
her portrayal of those violent men who fought to shape that
revolution to their purposes. Walk with her down a street of
London where the buildings remind her of the men who lived in
them and she makes history take shape before our eyes.

She can become almost as excited about communities of
people, of races and nations. To her they have much the same
distinctiveness as individuals. She never quite can forget that she
herself embodies this kind of history. Though she has lived in
England most of her life, she takes the opportunities that come
her way to point out that she is only partly English, and that her
Scots and Anglo-Irish ancestry sets her apart. Reaching even
further into her past, she traces her father's ancestry back to its
origins in the Slavic enclave, the Wends, in eastern Germany, and
then, when she was in Yugoslavia, saw that same Slavic

appearance repeated in the men of Bosnia.

The men who came down to the markets from the upland villages all looked at me out of my father's face.
They had the same magnificent eyes under level brows, the same strong, dark hair and moustache, the high cheekbones, the straight nose, the tan skin. . . . [T]here was a like gauntness, and [my father] carried himself with the same air which these Bosnians had acquired through centuries spent in guerrilla warfare against the Turkish conqueror. He looked exotic, romantic, and a zealot.[16]

Her father conveyed in his appearance and air the experiences of his ancestors, his race, though he is removed in time and place from them. It seems an anomaly, but his daughter accepted it, just as she responded to the possibility, as she watched the assassination of King Alexander of Yugoslavia on a newsreel, that one could learn by other means than thoughtful observation. He could probe his racial memory as well. History, the memory of the race, and the attitudes of the individual blur here until they are almost indistinguishable, one from the other.

If we remove the individual, the nation and the race can still retain their distinctiveness and excitement for her. The history of France, the country she most consistently prefers above others, would have its uniqueness because it would be the experience of the French race, and would be as different in quality from German history or English history as French culture differs from that of Germany, the country for which she has the most persistent animus, or England, the country she knows and loves but is always willing to criticize. When Rebecca West returned to Yugoslavia with her husband in 1937, she told him that it was necessary that they make the journey because she was taking him to a country "where everything was comprehensible, where the mode of life was so honest that it put an end to perplexity."[17] It is as if, among all the countries she knew, she had finally found that one for which she was seeking, and in a most unlikely place. For her the mode of life she witnessed there exemplified the spirit of the race, the precious residue of a history that had removed much of the dross she found in other countries, including England. These countries, she felt, had never experienced the fire that refines to the extent the Southern Slavs had. West's excitement about Yugoslavia carried

her through over 1,200 pages of examination of their mode of
life, more than she had written about anything else, before she
felt she had done it justice.

West makes of history an act of discovery, a stretching out to
comprehend, an adventurous journey into the past which is
never quite distinct and separate from the present moment. It is
most meaningful when it embodies people, when it approximates
myth.

VIII   St. Augustine

Rebecca West published three books— *St. Augustine* (1933), *A
Letter to a Grandfather* (1933), and *Black Lamb and Grey
Falcon* (1941)—in which she expresses more fully her sense of
the meaning and value of history. Each book is very different
from the other two. *St. Augustine* and *A Letter to a Grandfather*
are short; *Black Lamb and Grey Falcon* is huge and sprawling. *St.
Augustine* is a study of the man in his time, designed for popular
reading. *A Letter to a Grandfather* presents an impressionistic
reading of English history as Virginia Woolf might have done it
for a relatively sophisticated reader. *Black Lamb and Grey
Falcon* gives us great chunks of Yugoslavian history without
concern for their chronological order, set in the author's reading
of what they mean and what they foretell.

West's biography of St. Augustine was one in a series of short,
popular biographies published by Peter Davies. The series
includes many distinguished authors, among them Stephen
Leacock, who wrote on Mark Twain, and André Maurois, whose
subject was Voltaire. West's biography offers the starting point
of that historical continuum she thought might help explain the
troubled world she lived in. She states in her preface that she
wanted to describe Augustine's personal life and to place it in its
historical context. She did not consider it her task to present his
theology except in so far as it was relevant to an explanation of
what he was, both as an individual and as that historical
phenomenon, the first modern man, other scholars already had
recognized. West had another reason for writing this book. As a
young girl she had been attracted to St. Augustine; whatever
work of his she read, his *Confessions,* his letters, his *City of God,*
she found it an absorbing experience. She sensed in him a
kindred spirit.

She began the biography with a long quotation by Cyprian, Bishop of Carthage, in which he describes the decay of the Roman Empire. She used the quotation to set the context in which she wants us to see St. Augustine. It reads in part:

The world has now grown old, and does not abide in that strength in which it formerly stood. . . . The husbandman is failing in the fields, the sailor at sea, and the soldier in the camp. Honesty is no longer to be found in the market place, nor justice in the law courts, nor good craftsmanship in art, nor discipline in morals.[18]

She quotes this as a description of the world of St. Augustine, but it evokes the same sinking sensation she felt for the Europe of her day. Like hers, his world exhibited charm and culture. Again like hers, it was decaying from within and cowering before threatening, barbaric forces from without. In his world there was despair and there was also hope. If the old Roman order was collapsing, the new Christian faith was developing its first great social vitality. But in her world hope was not apparent, unless one was a convert to one of the new totalitarianisms. In them she found nothing that could serve as a new faith for her.

West describes both the despair and the hope of St. Augustine. She shows him caught up in the turmoil and eventual triumph of his struggle to master himself, his conversion to Christianity, and his final security in the hands of God. He realized only too well what was happening to his world and yet rose above it. Seeking answers to his uncertainties, he found them in a set of concepts that marks him as this first modern man. Accepting a basic dualism of matter and spirit in man, be believed that matter, especially if related to sex, is evil, that man's involvement in matter has made him sin, and that for this sin he must atone to an angry God by suffering and renouncing easy pleasure. This is basic to Christian thought, Catholic and Protestant alike, and while St. Augustine's emphasis on unity of religious and social effort helped establish Catholicism as the dominant religion of Western Europe for a thousand years, the authority he gave to such a concept as predestination supported Protestant Calvinism's later challenge to that Catholic unity. By examples like these, West bolsters her argument that St. Augustine's concept of man, his place in the universe and his relation to God, had a profound influence on the development of Western civilization through the two great phases of its religious development.

West's description of Augustine's world emphasizes its disorder, its violence, its schismatic impulses, and its agonies as it passed through a tremendous political and spiritual revolution. Augustine was born into a world still committed to the Pax Romana and died just before the Vandals laid siege to his city of Hippo. He lived to witness the Christian Church gain power, spiritual and temporal, and exercised that power himself, but he also saw it torn by powerful schisms that were destructive to the Church's unity. Before his conversion to the True Faith, he was a Manichean for nine years, believing then that he lived in a confusion of good and evil, light and dark, that he was made by Satan out of this confusion, and that his life was a struggle to sort each from the other. He abandoned this belief, and later fought against it, as he did against the other heresies of his time: Arianism (the belief that Christ is neither the eternal Son of God nor of the same substance), Pelagianism (the belief that there was no original sin and that the will is free and can attain righteousness), Donatism (the belief that only a righteous priest can administer a valid sacrament).

None of these heresies seems abhorrent. Each seems to have its basis in some truth of human nature, though it is not the Truth. Each has its appeal, its attractiveness. As West describes the disputes over these heresies, they were not just battles of words. They were struggles for the hearts and minds of men. They were attacks on both the authority of the Church and the civil order. The power of an idea, if it appealed to man's nature, could have the strength of armies. Nothing could counter it except the power of another idea set against it. In West's view, the character of the age of Augustine was determined as much by the struggle over these ideas as by any other factor. St. Augustine made himself one of the primary agents of this struggle. Much of the fascination West feels for him has its source here in this conflict of beliefs.

The theoretical assumptions about history West makes in this book are at least twofold. First, she accepts the concept that history is the consequence of what great men think and do. The intellect and personality of St. Augustine helped effect an historical revolution that without him would have taken a different form. Not just ideas are important. Unassociated with the force and color of a personality their significance can pass unnoticed, their relevance unmarked. This biography is evidence of West's preference for the impact and drama of the individual instead of the cumulation of more general data that characterizes the espousers of some other theories of history. No matter how far she may be carried by some exposition of an idea. she relates it to the human attribute that pulls the idea into the viable context of our mundane existence. So she can trace St. Augustine's thought through the intricacies of his doctrine, or describe his sense of ineffable transcendence as he experienced his greatest religious ecstasy, but never forget that he carried with him always something of his father's irascible, high-handed personality, or that he was torn between his idealization of woman, exemplified for him by his sainted mother, and his ardent passion for the sensual pleasure other women could give him. Which is to say that, however great the man, he partakes of our common humanity. West is enough a child of the nineteenth century to conceive of the possibility that in the sometime-future humanity may elevate itself to something better than what it now is, but that still, to use an Augustinian phrase, we are born *inter faeces et urinam.*

The second assumption about history present here is that a great man like Augustine may effect a change in the course of history but still be conditioned strongly by what is known and accepted in his day. Commitment to a spiritual life might equally have been his in another culture and era, but the uncertainties of a decaying Roman imperialism were in themselves compulsion enough to turn him from a social order that earlier would have provided a meaningful stability, and to direct him, instead, toward Christianity, that other force available to him, nascent, surgent, offering a different order and significance. It gave him a certainty of belief that enabled him to live with paradoxes and uncertainties, the characteristics of his age.

West seems here to assume that history is, as Thomas Carlyle proposed, a collection of biographies of great men. As she develops it, her illustration offers evidence that man thinking is more important than man doing. Though she never examines carefully the historical significance of the barbarian hordes sweeping down on Rome, she leaves the suggestion in the reader's mind that, do what they will, these barbarians will eventually be influenced by St. Augustine's thinking, and that he will, in the end, prevail.

IX   A Letter to a Grandfather

The second book of interest to one looking at West's perception of history is her forty-five-page essay published by the Hogarth Press in 1933 as No. 7 in a series called the Hogarth Letters. The authors of the Hogarth Letters, an impressive list of writers, were given great freedom in their choice of subjects.

Rebecca West entitled her essay *A Letter to a Grandfather* and used it as a vehicle for surveying what she saw as the spiritual changes that had characterized English culture from the Middle Ages to the twentieth century. She traced these changes through the members of one family, the Beauchamps, choosing one from each historical era and making him a perceptive assessor of that era. Each of these individuals had his vision of man, of man's nature and his relation to God. To receive their visions the Beauchamps stand "in front of the thing which is hidden to all other people all their lives long, and look at it as much as it wants to be looked at, and take just what it wants to give one."[19] The device West employed permits her to comment symbolically on the historical developments of Great Britain through selected personae, each with his individual bias, each schooled in a medium of cultural expression thought to be characteristic of his era. So the representative of one generation can be a builder of churches, another can be a connoisseur of painting, or a poet, or scientist, whatever activity West thinks appropriate for that moment in Britain's cultural history.

One assumption about history to be derived from this device is obvious: time is characterized by change. But West puts controls on temporal flux by using the constant of the Beauchamp family. She adds support to this constant by emphasizing certain symbolic objects as they occur in each age and pointing out their interrelatedness.

As in her *St. Augustine,* here also she characterizes human nature as in part divine, in part bestial, and she permits man neither to deny nor separate himself entirely from either. About man's ability to improve himself or his condition West has little optimism, so her history demonstrates little discernible change for the better, and what might be seen as improvement is only an avoidance of reality. She does present man as having a chance to obtain the best that life can give him, but only if he understands and accepts his existence in its actuality. Here sometimes history can help him by providing him with examples from the past which, if he interprets them properly, make clearer the obscurities and distortions of the present.

The author of the letter begins her historical survey with the medieval world of Philippe de Beauchampe, who built an abbey to commemorate his vision. His world she sees exemplified in the "harsh and solid and real architecture"[20] of the abbey he created, that in its height and breadth made one think of a man outstretched in pain on a cross, creating "a tense and interesting pattern worked on the surface of infinity."[21] The image is one of expiation and agony, but Beauchamp's abbey the writer of the letter has seen can only suggest it because little but ruins remain, except for the dovecote where abides the symbol of the spirit which both sustains us and makes us suffer.

The early Renaissance offered a softer, less painful prospect to the Beauchamp who was privy counsellor to Henry VIII. The Virgin Mary was there as an intercessor, a whole host of saints were available as liaisons to the divine Godhood, and everything seemed more accessible and pleasurable. The Reformation destroyed many of these comforts, thus causing Richard Beauchamp, a religious poet of that era, to turn to the art of argument as his instrument of belief.

The eighteenth century of Geoffrey Beauchamp, country gentleman, also believed in the value of argument, though it was not what it claimed to be, an age of reason. Like any other era it was moved by faith, but it encompassed such extremes of benevolence and self-indulgence, of elegance and poverty, of reason and sentiment, of humanistic self-sufficiency and mystic aspiration to the divine, that it seems an absurd paradox based on a confusion of spiritual and ethical values with an impulse to stress the will, that instrument of the ethical world, and give it play in the spiritual world where it could only confuse man's perception of his relation to the eternal. So it was a troubled age, contradictory, a fractured intellectual puzzle, an age that ended in revolution fired by passions that the century had tried to deny. Arthur Beauchamp saw his vision of it in the Place de la Republique, where he witnessed the death of Louis XVI, last of the Capets.

This giving of one's self to one's passions was not lost on the

succeeding generation of George Beauchamp, who hated Byron
because he detected that what for the earlier revolutionaries
was a surrender to passion became for his and Byron's generation
a self-conscious absorption in sensation. Such an emphasis
presented dangers because it cut short the process by which the
sensory experience was received and interpreted by an intelligence responsive to human tradition, but it did serve the purpose
of bringing humanity back to a reality basic to any later
summation of human experience. It transcended, as well, that
tendency of the nineteenth century to confuse the sensuous with
a fussy morality. To an extent poets avoided this quagmire, but
scientists did even better, for they concentrated on the facts of
man's past and his environment, thus reviving an interest in the
unity of experience and a belief that it should be tested to make
sure it is true. In doing so, they set up a safeguard against man's
tendency to deceive himself. However, her Victorian grandfather's vision, his sense of life's unity cannot be fully interpreted
by the author because she does not know precisely what it was,
in part because this scientist grandfather put it in a language,
mathematics, which she does not understand, but in part too
because there is not enough distance in time to give her
perspective.

She has even less understanding of her father, for with him she
could not even speak; he was too closely identified with her
developing awareness of human nature in its darker aspects, its
susceptibility to disease and perversion, its capacity, even in the
child conceived in love, to grow jealous of its parental origins.
And if these characteristics of human nature were not enough to
make her critical of her father and his generation, there lay
between them the waste of the First World War. The world she
inherited lacks order and healthy, life-giving qualities.

Tradition has been thrown out of the window by all parties, even those
who pretend to be traditionalists. Can the earth have seen such idiots as
those who declare that they want to submit to the authority of the
Roman Catholic Church, not because they believe in its supernatural
revelation, but because they dislike the disorder of life lived without
authority?. . . .But they are not more fatuous than those of the Left
Wing, who have thrown the whole tradition of economic idealism out of
the window, and babble of nothing but Russia.[22]

As seen in her vision, the contemporary world becomes a merry-go-round named "Le Dragon" whose attendant is a tall, weary Negro in worn scarlet evening clothes and carrying a cane he uses to direct the riders of the merry-go-round to their proper seats. He expresses derision for his customers and signals the end of their ride with an erotic gesture, all done with perfect timing and grace, while from his face seems to fly forth a dove just as surely as it did from the dovecote of the medieval abbey.

What the author concludes is that hers is an age of iron, an "appalling century,"[23] a waste land, a fated turn on an amusement wheel, but this realization she would not bemoan. Rather, its bareness, its lack of pretence, makes it possible for her to see it in its actual form, which, to return to her earlier image, meant that her generation, outstretched in a tension similar to that of the medieval man on his cross, made the same attempt to know, and feel everything, though caught in the confines of ignorance and isolation common to all men. The great danger lay with those of her generation who hankered to submit themselves to authority, whether they be the neohumanists emitting the musty odor of a long-dead past against whom she turned so violently, or the apologists for the proletarian dictatorships of the left or the right. Between them she made little distinction, since the similarities were more striking than the contrasts and both versions resulted from the working classes, shackled as they were to the industrial machine, being cut off from those cultural traditions that formerly had given them character and made for form and significance and civilization.

Though the author of the letter began with the assumption that something had gone awry in the last two or three centuries, she finds no coherent order in the historical panorama she presents; if it were there, the visions of her ancestors would not be the unique, unforeseen revelations they became. But she does try to find general patterns that suffice for a relation of this phenomenon to that, as when she restates Vico's theory of history as a series of gradually ascending cycles with their promise that if we discern their pattern we can improve this time over the previous cycle. The same assumption of recurrence is to be found in that other pattern West describes elsewhere, the movement back and forth between the polarities of Romanticism and Classicism. The theory of Vico, as interpreted here, moves through phases of determinism and free will; the Romantic-Classic theory West sees as a fluctuation between sensation and cognition. The two theories seem to be variant interpretations of the same general phenomenon, and, insofar as she can accept the theory, West appears consistent in her preference for the free will–cognitive–Classic phase to the deterministic-sensating-Romantic phase. A pattern of opposing alternatives which West does consistently accept are the polarities of life and death and the paradox that man is attracted to both. Sometimes history shows him choosing one, sometimes the other. For West the choice is never in doubt; those forces which energize and sustain life are preferable to those which debilitate and urge us toward death. This concept had special relevance for her as she wrote this letter because she could see Europe blindly slipping into a death frenzy that to her even then seemed inevitable. The Hitlers and Mussolinis would have their way because those who could stop them had neither the vision nor the will to do so.

So the 1930s would pass, marked by the aggressive fanaticism of the right and the "fatuity and confusion"[24] of the left. England vacillated; France crouched behind its defense line. Spain degenerated into "a kind of war brothel where Left Wingers could drop in and have a little military excitement without binding themselves by any profound relationship to the experiment."[25] The actions of the Left Wingers were bad enough, but they were made worse by "the alacrity with which the Right Wing turned the house of a decent nation into that brothel."[26] Germany thrust its strength against the increasingly flabby borders of its neighbors, first on the west as it moved into the Saar, then, with its *Drang nach Osten,* to the east at whatever spot it sensed the greatest weakness. Italy, with less consistency and greater recklessness, flung itself into one adventure after another.

All of this is appalling, but in her letter the author will not leave it at that. Her vision has given her strength to live with the truth.

My generation has long known it lived in winter, but it has deplored it. I no longer do. Now the trees are bare, now one can see the form of the land. . . . We can embrace it in its completeness, we can accept the truth."[27]

X   Black Lamb and Grey Falcon

Rebecca West made another, much more ambitious effort to understand what was happening to her world. She chose as her subject Yugoslavia, a part of that area, the Balkans, which through all of her lifetime had been labeled "the powderkeg of Europe." She realized that events in the Balkans had affected all Europe, including her. Yet she knew nothing of the area, which meant, she concluded, that she did not know her own destiny. She had other, equally compelling reasons for making this effort. The Southern Slavs were attractive to her. They were Slavic, which for her meant that they were interested in the significance of things; they thought, they argued, they questioned ultimate purposes. They were different, yet they seemed familiar; she found them compatible. They had a history, long and complex, yet they were relatively untouched by the debasing cultural effects of what Rebecca West thought to be the source of twentieth-century Europe's problems, the Industrial Revolution. They held there in uneasy relationship three major religions, two Christian, one Moslem. The two Christian religions, the Roman Catholic Church and the Orthodox Church, expressed between them a range of Christian thought and practice as great as all that St. Augustine had witnessed or thought of. She saw there the conflict between the determination of old empires to conquer, to dominate, and equally old aspirations of races and peoples to be free, to be their own masters. She found there in miniature the bitter, disappointing history of man's struggle to improve himself. She found there also that the survivors of that history could still show her much she admired. They seemed to her the quintessence of what is feminine and masculine. She saw it in their appearance and in the modes of their lives. They exhibited an awareness that life is good, that it offers enjoyment for those who seek it honorably, and that it offers wisdom as well if one goes in quest of it. *Black Lamb and Grey Falcon* is her record of her quest.

Though *Black Lamb and Grey Falcon* has significant elements of history in it, formally it is not a history. It is a travelogue; its basic form is determined by space, not time; the author describes as often as she narrates. The book presents the journey West and her husband took through Yugoslavia during the spring of 1937. She had been there the year previous on a lecture tour and had found the people and landscape so attractive she persuaded her husband to return with her so they could share the experience together. Thus the segments of history she relates depend for their sequence on the itinerary of a planned journey. History becomes an explanatory extension of what they saw. The physical evidence of past thought and action—the statue, the church, the battlefield, the memorial plaque—acquires a projection into that moment of present actuality which, as West recounts its history, possesses a tangible reality: the past comprehended in the presence of that which still exists but yet is a part of that past.

If West had written *Black Lamb and Grey Falcon* in the nineteenth century her book would have been described as a collection of travel sketches and its title could more characteristically be what West described it to be on her title page, *A Journey through Yugoslavia,* or it could have been *Sketches of the Balkans,* or *From Slovenia to Macedonia.* As it is, West has modified to suit her purposes a literary form that had its greatest popularity in the nineteenth century and that she admired greatly when practiced by her contemporary, H. M. Tomlinson. An earlier author like Henry James had used the form as a device for registering his personal impressions and sensibilities, not for sketching a general view of history. Writers of James's generation also used the travel sketch as an apprenticeship to the craft of writing, and the techniques they perfected there they later subsumed into their fiction. West used this literary form for recording both a personal and a public history, and brought it to perfection comparatively late in her career. There is yet another distinction. For James and his contemporaries the term "sketch" carried with it the connotation of pictorial quality; they called this quality "picturesqueness." West sought a different quality and identified it by a different term, "visibility." To her "visibility" meant some expression of human existence that was both striking in its individual quality and revelatory of some more general and basic characteristic of a culture or a life. What she sees tends to resolve itself into a scene, not a picture. It has energy, it moves. It is no longer conditioned by the nineteenth century's penchant for the sentimental, the morbid, and the static. In the congenial atmosphere of Yugoslavia where West felt she needed only to stand in readiness for this "visibility" to make itself apparent, she could lean out of herself, she could stand before the vision that Yugoslavia presented to her, and if she tried, she could understand what it meant. As she discovered, Yugoslavia seemed to lean out in response, showing her what she desired to know, sharing with her its history and its unique vision of life.

The method she uses here for presenting history is one particularly well suited to an aesthetic sensibility because it requires an alert, informed response to sensory phenomena. To one less responsive, less willing to open oneself to new experience, the method can degenerate into invidious comparisons. Someone not so aware of man's urge to transform his most valued concepts and memorable events into some more permanent form would see little there of value. He would dismiss it as the rubbish of history, as something alien, without significance, unworthy of his consideration It is this stultifying alternative, this negation of Rebecca West's response to the Yugoslavian experience that largely justifies her giving such prominence in her book to Gerda, the German wife of her Yugoslavian friend and guide Constantine, for Gerda is presented as persistently showing contempt for much that seems most significant to West. What West values in these people is reduced by Gerda to a titter and the explanation, "They are such savages."[28]

There is hardly an experience West describes in *Black Lamb and Grey Falcon* to which she reacted with disdain or revulsion. Like the Beauchamps in *A Letter to a Grandfather,* each of whom stood before his vision until he understood it, and like Princip, the assassin of Franz Ferdinand, in whom she sympathetically sensed the ability to accept wholeheartedly each experience in the hope that it would reveal to him what it could of ultimate truth. West too wanted to examine each object and event so that she could learn its nature and meaning and relation to what else she knows of life. What she did see seemed at first to be contrasts and paradoxes. She saw vital, healthy people caught in a geographic and political situation that entrapped and destroyed them. She saw complexes of languages and cultures and religions, one overlaying the other, with only a general South Slavic identity to keep it all together. Yet in each phenomenon she looked at she found the possibility of enlightenment: viewing the corpse of Prince Lazar, who died over five centuries before, she could reach out her finger and touch his hand; looking at the

grave of Princip, she could remember the answers he had given
to his interrogators in the record of his trial; exploring the
accommodations the residents of Split had made to living in the
ruins of Diocletian's palace, she saw more clearly what that
ruined grandeur had done to their spirits; standing at the
Orthodox Easter service in the church at Skoplje, she saw in vivid
pageantry the value of commemorating in ritual the important
reoccurring events of our lives. So she found it wherever she
went, wandering in the markets, meeting strangers on the road in
the hotels, observing the costumes and manners, savoring the
food and drink. Each object, each experience, offered the
possibility of a revelation in itself.

Whether or not the itinerary of their journey was so designed,
it supported the purposes West set for herself in her book. The
journey began with a train ride through Austria into Croatia, that
part of Yugoslavia most influenced by a familiar Western culture,
Austria, and thus mostly easily comprehended. Observing the
Germans traveling with her enabled her to describe what she
conceived to be their character and its relation to the developing
crisis in Europe, so a compelling reason is established for the
journey of exploration to come. After seeing Zagreb and its
environs, she and her husband moved down the Dalmatian Coast
where the Roman, Catholic, and Venetian influences were most
evident, again cultural influences comparatively accessible to
the Western European mind. After this preparation, they moved
inland to Sarajevo, where much of the history that created the
Yugoslavia of 1937 could be recounted. Then by moving east to
Belgrade, they went back into the past of old Serbia where the
spirit that fostered the creation of Yugoslavia was most apparent.
There, as well, the Slavic and Moslem influences became more
pronounced, influences which were intensified as West and her
husband journeyed south to Macedonia, a place so special to her
she felt compelled to explain that it was the most beautiful
country she had even seen; it "is the country I have always seen
between sleeping and waking.[29] From there they moved through
the Montenegrin Mountains, whose fastnesses had helped sustain
both the possibility of the Yugoslavia Rebecca West saw and the
Yugoslavia that emerged from World War II, on to the Adriatic
just in time to see frightening evidence of German and Italian
agents preparing for Italy's move into Albania. So the journey

was a movement from the familiar to the unfamiliar and back, from the present into the past and back into an even more contemporary present. It began and concluded with disagreeable evidences of man's perversity, but in its progress it opened one vista after another of man's nobility and benignity, his determination to rescue beauty from chaos.

Reading *Black Lamb and Grey Falcon* as history, one would do well to begin with West's concept of natural man. She describes him as self denying, not out of asceticism, but from an unwillingness to give of himself to joy or pleasure. He holds back from commitments to friendship or love and the dues they exact in mercy and patience and understanding. He is churlish. He is mean.[30] West here repudiates Rousseau's concept that natural man is noble, which, stated this starkly, seems in need of qualification. There are many ways of not being noble. West's version places natural man in a particularly disagreeble, withdrawn nullity. Nothing issues from it except a sour wish for death.

West so defined natural man while explaining why the Manichean heresy had attracted so many Christians to it. If one takes the passage out of that context and reads it simply as a characterization of man in his natural state, then one can assume that this is man unaffected by history. History should then become a civilizing force, fostering in man those social attributes that enable him to function as a vitalizing agent. It should prompt him to encourage life-sustaining patterns of culture. But West presented her concept of natural man in the context of a heresy she thought induced these mean characteristics in man. Since the Manichean heresy is a significant part of the history of Christianity, history cannot be seen simply as ameliorative. It allows, or even induces, man to revert to his natural state just as surely as it encourages him toward a civilized state. History is like West's characterization of life, "that sail flapping in the contrary winds of the universe."[31]

The history of Yugoslavia that West presents in *Black Lamb and Grey Falcon* illustrates this ambivalent effect. The two great forces that promoted civilization among the South Slavs were race and religion. The Slavic tribes that came into this area in the declining years of the Roman Empire brought with them democratic traits that as a group they still exhibit today. This helps explain their tremendous pride in being what they are as

well as their determination to fight off foreign domination, but it
is a reason as well why their long history has been characterized
by their continual quarreling with each other that has left them
easier victims for the Turkish, Austrian, and Russian drives to
empire than they otherwise would have been. Religion gave
them a way of organizing their lives, of imposing ritual on their
otherwise disorganized and deprived existences. The Orthodox
Church in particular gave them an art that West characterized as
"a calligraphy for the expression of man's graver experiences
which makes all other arts seem a little naive or gross."[32]
Religion's detrimental effect was that it helped create and
perpetuate the schisms that plague the South Slavs even today.
On the whole, however, the influence of race and religion on the
South Slavs has been positive. The great negative influence has
been empire, always empire.

In their contrasting histories, the Serbs and Croats demonstrate the alternatives that time and place made available to
them. The history of the Serbs shows them facing east, to
Byzantium, which gave them the Orthodox Church but made
them feel, as St. Augustine felt at Hippo, like an outpost of a
declining splendor. The first great advance for Serbia was the
200-year reign of the Nemanya dynasty, which West compares to
the Tudor period in English history. It ended with the defeat of
the Serbs by the Turks at the Battle of Kossovo in 1389. The
Nemanyas gave Serbia a saint, St. Sava, who founded the Serbian
Orthodox Church, a hero king, Stephen Dushan, who was
crowned emperor of the Serbs, Bulgars, Greeks, and Albanians,
and a hero martyr, Prince Lazar, remembered in ballad, who
dreamed of a grey falcon and died the next day defending his
country. Four centuries of Turkish domination followed. The
Serbs paid their tribute to the Porte and were given in return the
Janissaries, their own children who were taken from them and
then sent back as soldiers schooled to dominate and terrorize
them. Only in the nineteenth century did the Serbs slowly win
their freedom back. Again heroes emerge, Karageorge the
warrior and Milos Obrenovitch the diplomat, and again Serbia
advanced, choosing its rulers from the descendants of these two
heroes. Too often the ascendence of the Obrenovitchs meant a
regression into meanness which finally culminated in the
slaughter of Alexander and his wife, Draga, by a group of
officers. The Karageorges offered something truer to the spirit

of the Serbs. It was Alexander Karageorgevitch, great-grandson of Karageorge, who led Serbia through World War I, became King of Yugoslavia, and died the victim of a terrorist in Marseilles, France, in 1934. With a Karageorge still as its king, Yugoslavia followed the tradition of Serbia in its defiance of Hitler in World War II, even though its leaders knew it meant defeat. West cannot speak too highly of the Serbs' will to freedom. The genius of their history she characterized as "harsh, potent, realist, daemonic, furtive and nocturnal."[33] Examined one by one, these qualities do not all appear to be ennobling, but given Serbia's history, they make the aggregate required by the Serbs to secure that which they most ardently sought, their freedom to work out their own destiny in terms of their own nature.

Rebecca West summarized her distinction between the Serbs and Croats as follows: "History has made lawyers of the Croats, soldiers and poets of the Serbs. It is an unhappy divergence."[34] The Croats were "lawyers" because they looked west to the Roman Catholic Church and north and west to Hungary and Austria. They put their hopes for salvation in the Roman Catholic Church and their political belief in treaties with Hungary and Austria. Their history begins fairly enough. They had the Roman Catholic faith and they had their own king. This condition continued until the eleventh century when their last king died leaving no heir to the throne. The Croatian nobles fought among themselves until in exhaustion they chose an outsider, Coloman, King of Hungary. His realm became the dual kingdom of Hungary and Croatia. When he died the crown passed through a strange series of foreign, mostly indifferent successors, one of them selling the Dalmatian Croats to Venice for 100,000 ducats, another reducing Croatia to a subordinate relation with Hungary. As the Turks moved north through Serbia, they bypassed Croatia and defeated the Hungarians at the Battle of Mohacs in 1526. Surrounded on three sides by the Turks, the Croats turned in desperation to Austria, offering the Croatian throne to Ferdinand of Hapsburg. In return Austria made Croatia into what were called the Military Confines within which every male between sixteen and sixty was part of a standing army whose duty it was to defend the Austrian Empire. As the oppressions of the Croat increased their nationalism grew, but also, strangely, their devotion to the Hapsburgs. They were used as a pawn of empire; to appease a rebellious Hungary, Maria Theresa broke her legal promises to the Croats and made them an annexed territory of Hungary. There they remained until 1848, when Kossuth carried Hungary again into rebellion against Austria. In defense of the Hapsburgs, the Croats defeated the Hungarians. They were rewarded, not with their freedom, but by being made directly subject to Austria again. So it remained until World War I. Out of all of these shattered hopes only one great name emerges, the wise, sweet spirited Bishop Strossmayer, who did what he could to secure some measure of self determination for the Croats.

The centuries the Croats spent worrying over legal documents that seemed too often to turn into scraps of paper gave them that argumentative stance of aggrieved self evaluation that led West to characterize them as lawyers. They were in fact great warriors, but they put their faith where history proved it was not justified. Their history finally taught them to look suspiciously at authority wherever it came from outside Croatia. When Yugoslavia was formed and Serbian Belgrade became its capitol, the Croats' disaffection focused on it. In her journey West could hardly find a Croat who did not complain about the government in Belgrade, and one of the last sights she saw in Yugoslavia was an antigovernment demonstration in Zagreb. When World War II came, the history of the Croats and the sense it had induced in them of their alienation from other South Slavs brought them closer to sympathy with the Axis than any other group in Yugoslavia. World War II brought not only the Germans, it brought as well an undeclared civil war that obliterated whole communities, mostly in Croatia and Serbia, because the politics or ethnic backgrounds of these communities were different from their neighbors. West foresaw clearly enough what outsiders could do to the South Slavs. She foretold less accurately what the Yugoslavs could do to each other.

These histories of the Serbs and the Croats show them united in their desire for self-determination. Both of them were brave and resolute. Where they differed was in their perception of how they could attain that freedom. The accidents of geography and the burdens of their differing histories forced Serbia into centuries of bondage to the Turks, but kept the Serbs determined and independent of mind in their struggle, while Croatia sought that same freedom by allying itself with those

Rebecca West considered to be its natural enemies and found itself as a result less sure of its own uniqueness and value. The fatal moment for Serbia is accepted in balladry as the death of Prince Lazar at Kossovo; for Croatia it was the decision to accept Coloman, King of Hungary, as its king. Yet what they both sought was good and basically it was the same.

One conclusion the reader can draw from West's history of Yugoslavia is that nations, like individuals, should be free. She recognized that World War I had done this for many small peoples in Europe: the Finns, the Czechs and Slovacs, the Latts and Esths, the Serbs and Croats. She described them as like young men stretching themselves after a long sleep. To them it was bliss what for a long time had been only a dream. But it became possible, she thought, because they had remained true to themselves. They had not sold their souls. They had not lost their identities.

This is a magnificent achievement, and it needs to be celebrated, as West does here, but it is too simple and too optimistic a concept of history for her to leave it at that. What she found in Croatia would, in itself, have made her uneasy. Nor does it answer the question why she gave her book the title *Black Lamb and Grey Falcon*. The answer to that choice lies in the horrors of this recital of the past that made the writing of it at times an agony for her. Too often it is a history of death. She begins the book with the death of Alexander Karageorgevitch, follows it with three other assassinations, then moves to Archduke Franz Ferdinand, then to the frenzied butchering of Alexander Obrenovitch and Draga Mashim, then back in history to Prince Lazar's death. The two dominant symbols of the book, the gray falcon and the black lamb, both depend for their significance on their relation to death—death and rebirth, perhaps, but still death.

The gray falcon symbolizes life after death. It appeared to Prince Lazar on the eve of the Battle of Kossovo, the battle that determined Serbia's subjugation to the Turks for centuries, centuries in which the memory of that battle was preserved and cherished in the folk epic it produced. The falcon promised Prince Lazar that, if he were to die on the battlefield, his soul would be saved. The prince chose the exaltation of death and defeat to the possibility of life and freedom for his people. And yet, in the words of the ballad:

> All was holy, all was honourable
> And the goodness of God was fulfilled.[35]

When in World War II the leaders of Yugoslavia refused to capitulate to the demands of Hitler, the people, knowing this act meant invasion and defeat, went about reciting these lines.

The black lamb too is an ambivalent symbol. The image of a man cradling a lamb in his arms recurs through the book. West sees him, young and vigorous, as he appears unexpectedly in the door of a bar in Belgrade, a peasant cradling the lamb in his arms. She sees a similar young man on the battlefield at Kossovo. She sees also another man, this one old and frail, carrying what is this time a sacrificial lamb on the Sheep's Field near Skoplje, where on St. George's Eve barren women had come for centuries to participate in this annual fertility sacrifice. Rebecca West witnessed this sacrifice. What she saw revolted her, but still she accepted it as a timeless act that exemplified something basic in man's nature.

I knew this rock well. I had lived under the shadow of it all my life. All our Western thought is founded on this repulsive pretence that pain is the proper price of any good things.[36]

Out of death, life. Through death one may find life. Even the entry into this life is uncertain, hazardous, painful.

Whatever else West found in Yugoslavia, whatever nobility and triumph of the human spirit, she saw that spirit darkened by the presence of death. If anything or anyone transcends its shadow, his achievement takes the form of a legacy to the race, not to the individual. An occasional great man like Bishop Strossmeyer emerges triumphant because he leaves a spiritual legacy, but he is one of the few from whom light emanates in this history. In most men the dark prevails, and the significance of these men seems clearest in their deaths.

A concept of history so oriented to death cannot be optimistic. It is couched, rather, in terms that William Faulkner would have understood. Man must endure, and he may prevail. He questions and finds few answers, he is in doubt and discovers little certainty. It is a concept not unlike the state of mind of the old woman whom Rebecca West and her husband met high in the mountains of Montenegro. Refusing an offer of help, the old woman explained:

"I am walking about to try to understand why all this has happened. If I had to live, why should my life have been like this? If I walk about up here where it is very high and grand it seems to me I am nearer to understanding it."[37]

This old woman is as effective and appealing an image of the human situation as West's earlier image of the medieval man racked on a cross. Man may be weak, but he questions and tries to understand. West also felt ineffectual, but she, like the old woman, had journeyed to a high, remote place because she thought that there she too might find answers that she could not find elsewhere.

At the beginning and end of her book Rebecca West wrote that she was examining the past of Yugoslavia in an effort to understand why Europe had arrived at the brink of World War II. She wanted to describe what she, a woman from Britain, understood to be the causes of this inevitable catastrophe. This committed her, she realized, to an inquiry into the basics of humanity. The reason she did not use the history she knew best, British history, was that its relative order and stability did not seem to her typical of the European experience. She could have turned to the more turbulent, unstable histories of Germany or Italy, since the forces of anarchy and destruction she saw loose in Europe were generated in these countries, but those histories offered her no alternative, only a plunge deeper into the purgatory where she already was. Yugoslavia fit her purpose better. The proletarian dictators of Germany and Italy and the political putrefaction they induced threatened to contaminate all of Europe. That would mean the subjugation of Britain and Yugoslavia alike. Rebecca West has never shown any desire to fawn before or run with power, so as an evidence of her own basic impulses, if for no other reason, she must respond favorably to a threatened Yugoslavia, a country without great power, but brave in its defiance of the seeming inevitable.

With nothing stable in the present to sustain her, she had turned to the past and had searched there for fundamentals which could carry her in spirit beyond the impending catastrophe. Though *Black Lamb and Grey Falcon* was for its author "an unendurably horrible book to have to write,"[38] she emerged from the experience with the conviction that at least two factors could change man from the creature who, from the evidence of her interpretation of history, seemed irredeemable.

Art was one of these factors. To create art was to relive
experience, and by that reliving to alter the experience and
arrive at its true significance. West makes the high claim of art
that it gave man the means of understanding life and controlling
his destiny. The other factor was not an activity of man; it was
the element of unpredictability in his existence. How could
unpredictability be beneficial? With a suggestion of nineteenth-
century optimism, West reverses our expectations. She saw
unpredictability as that positive possibility that man has unexpected resources and potentials which, in the pressure of the
worst of circumstances, could forge a heroism distinctively his.
When history predicted that which was too painful to contemplate, some unforeseen element could intrude to ameliorate the
situation.

For West, art and the unpredictability of history added up to a
glimpse of hope in 1938. In the immediacy of World War II she
did not seek further assurance; it was enough to observe the
nobility of the Yugoslav and British people during the war and to
see the possibility of survival. She concluded her study of history
almost as if she feared what she had found and was reacting as
she thought man had reacted throughout history. Man, she
argued, fears knowledge. He may seek it when he is ignorant, but
he is frightened by the uncertainty and change it causes.
Civilizations rise and fall with his anxieties. But she did want to
know, and her search through history convinced her that the
present is the living past. If we know that past, we have some
assurance of not misjudging the present.

What had she learned? She had learned that if one did not
know the past he was apt to make mistakes. Her study of history
stimulated conservative assumptions: the value of past precedent, of custom and tradition. It fostered as well a sense of a
continuum; history is rhythm, a movement among perennially
basic ideas, a fluctuation between contrasting responses to the
human situation. West is not a doctrinaire; she is a skeptic, but
not a determinist. Any willingness she may have to advocate
man's ability to ameliorate his condition by a process of
intellectual enlightenment is tempered by her awareness of his
willingness to follow his dark urges. She reads history as a record
of the whole human effort, not just of that part involving political
strategies or economic forces. If she does schematize history, she

does so by stressing ideas which seem to her often to dominate the movement of history. But ideas are produced by human beings, and one returns to the abiding interest in humanity as that humanity is exemplified by the individual in his wondrous uniqueness and by his affiliative bonds with others. For her, not power, not pleasure, not self-abnegation, not even order, but freedom and wisdom seem to be those goals most desired. They helped sustain her through the dark night of World War II.

CHAPTER 4

Analyst of Traitors

I   *The Traitor as New Political Phenomenon*

REBECCA West began her study of traitors for what would seem to be an irrelevant reason; paper was short in post-World War II England. There was not enough space in the newspapers to report adequately the court trials of those British subjects who had defected to Nazi Germany. West wanted that record kept; she recognized the importance of this phenomenon of the times and wanted people to examine it while it was on view, not years later when it had become history. Others also urged her to keep the record. So she became a frequenter of the law courts and soon produced a series of articles which appeared in the *New Yorker* in late 1945 and early 1946. Later in 1946 her interest carried her to the Nuremberg trials which she also reported for the *New Yorker* and the *London Daily Telegraph*. Even later her interest took her to the trials of those who had betrayed scientific secrets and military intelligence to Communist Russia. The record she has kept of those treasonous activities is both valuable and unique.

West was, however, not satisfied to be just a reporter. She took the next step and tried to answer the question "Why?" in an essay she entitled "The Meaning of Treason," published in *Harper's* in 1947. Here she attempted to define as well as to describe what she had observed. This essay served her as both title and central statement for her book *The Meaning of Treason* which she compiled from her reports and published in the same year.

For her the traitor appeared to be another manifestation of the same social and political malaise she had identified with the anarchists she had examined already in *Black Lamb and Grey Falcon*. The anarchists she analyzed in that book attacked authority by assassinating those in whom that authority resided. The traitors she examined here sapped the strength of authority, using propaganda, deception, and spying as their weapons. The anarchists were murderers; the traitors were more apt to be liars and thieves. At their worst the anarchists manifested a repulsive, gratuitous violence endemic in the rootless, unprincipled totalitarianism threatening to engulf Europe. The traitors seeped from the same source and were at least as insidious, for they acted as a corrosive, eating away basic concepts that hold human communities together.

If one remembers that in 1912 West entered the public scene by what at that time was conceived by many to be a rebellious act, her violent verbal attacks on a government that denied her something she thought should be hers, one could assume that for her to brand as traitors other dissidents who at a later date were withholding their loyalty from a later version of that same government would require in her some change of attitude, some shift of conviction. Yet whatever adjustment she did make seems more apparent than real. In "The Meaning of Treason" she accepts, for example, the assumption that "the relationship between man and a fatherland is always disturbed by conflict, if either man or fatherland is highly developed,"[1] and goes even further to assert that "all men should have a drop or two of treason in their veins, if the nations are not to go soft like so many sleepy pears."[2] But this is the price to be paid for that imperative asset of any worthwhile society, the freedom of the individual. The problem for the individual is to balance his need for freedom against his devotion to his nation. The problem for the nation is to balance its need for order and security against the frustrations implicit in that ideal state "where all talents are generously recognized, all forgivable oddities forgiven, all viciousness quietly frustrated,"[3] and all graciousness honored. It was precisely because West as a young woman believed her talents and vital impulses were being frustrated that she reacted as hostilely to her government as she did. When her position improved, when she felt less threatened personally, she could view society and its relation to the individual with greater emotional equanimity and less violent rhetoric.

II *Nationalism versus Internationalism*

This does not mean, though, that she did not have to make some significant emotional adjustments. In her essay "The Meaning of Treason" she states that an important cause for the

development of these traitors was the rise between World Wars I
and II of the attitude that patriotism was somehow old-fashioned
and suspect, and that nationalism lay at the heart of Europe's ills.
Men of good will argued for a supernational brotherhood. They
maintained that nationalism promoted imperialism, so they
welcomed the disintegration of the Austro-Hungarian Empire, as
did West, for like her they found the concept of empire suspect.

But nationalism is not just a prelude to empire. It has its roots
deep in the aspirations that motivated the revolutionary surge at
the end of the eighteenth century. It fostered the ethnic unity of
Italy and Germany in the nineteenth century and was an
informing principle of the Treaty of Versailles, in which new
national entities were created throughout central and eastern
Europe at the expense of the imperialist urges of Austria,
Germany, and Russia. So it had its advocates.

In counterargument, those who found nationalism suspect
argued that patriotism too often became jingoism. They pointed
to the systems of colonies Western Europe had developed, of
Russian expansionism under both the czars and the Communists,
of the constantly shifting borders of Europe, each one an area
where conflicting national interests festered, poisoning relations
between nations, stimulating aggressive impulses. They dreamed
of a federated Europe that would obviate the need for mutual
destruction in the name of national gain or honor.

West came down solidly for nationalism, which she conceived
to be "a special devotion of a people to its own material and
spiritual achievements."[4] For her, nationalism was the logical
extension of a simple truth; "that we live outward from the
center of a circle and that what is nearest to the center is most
real to us,"[5] but the circle is no larger than the boundaries of the
culture with which we identify. Those who attacked nationalism,
among whom she included "almost all contemporary left-wing
writers of this generation and the last,"[6] had, in her view,
forgotten the truth of what is most real to us because they had no
strong social locus and, as the products of a modern, urbanized,
technocratic society, had "lost their sense of spiritual as well as
material process."[7] They were adrift without those experiential
ties that promote valid judgments. They had substituted, instead,
a rationalism that may be used to promote a desirable ideal of
international brotherhood, but fails to aid in comprehending the
feasibility or the consequences of that ideal.

Who were these left-wing writers whom West held responsible for enervating British national pride? What writers were arguing "that it was pure superstition which required a man to feel any warmer emotion about his own land, race, and people than about any other?"[8] Among them one must count many of her associates from those early, exciting years in London. Certainly one of them was H. G. Wells, whose complex relationship with West would, at an earlier date, have given her pause before she could have made such a sweeping statement. Wells's associates in the Fabian Society meant less to her, but they exercised a dominance over English intellectual life that she, a young, ambitious aspirant to that life, would have had to come to terms with. This perhaps was made easier for her because she saw Wells as revolting against them with an almost instinctive realization that they were inimical to his sense of the richness and excitement of life. West's judgment of the Webbs and their more zealous disciples is harsh: "they lived in an atmosphere of negativism";[9] "the logical consequence of their bureaucratic theories was dictatorship";[10] they claimed a monopoly on the virtues they valued, "altruism and truthfulness and austerity . . . believing that they, and they alone, were the saviours of society."[11] Here hostility seems significant and deep-seated.

Some members of the Bloomsbury Group, closer to being West's contemporaries, could fit generally into the category she had set up, though their passion seems to be based more in aesthetics than politics. The humanism they advocated did contain, however, a passivity that had idealistic sources unconstrained by national boundaries. The group identified with W. H. Auden and Christopher Isherwood was of a generation a little younger than West, so though they still fit her characterization, they did not achieve a similar emotional hold on her.

H. G. Wells remains the principal, though not the most inimical, influence. Once she had severed her relationship with him, she could more easily reinforce in her own nature those values which to her had stood the test of experience. As late as 1939 she still thought of herself as left wing, but it was a left wing not unlike that of the earlier champion of women's rights, intensely democratic, intensely individualistic, aggressive.[12] It was a left wing that, given the chance to observe the social experiments in central and eastern Europe, was skeptical of untried social theories and was unwilling to engage in any experiment that for some supposedly utopian national end employed questionable means, usually at the expense of the free individual. It was a left wing that would fight Hitler and oppose the brutalities of Stalin. West is old-fashioned enough to champion the rights of man and hope that each of us can experience those rights within that cultural center we know and accept.

III   *Concepts of the Traitor*

Rebecca West's concept of the traitor is characteristically British. It embodies a traditional view, politically simple in its reliance on basic social values that reflect a stable community. Threats to this community originate from outside, not from within. Understanding may emerge, a judgment may be rendered, but forgiveness may not follow. She feels free to seek complexity in the psychological motivations of the traitors rather than in the political matrix of their community. West accepts that traditional concept of loyalty which is based on a personal relationship: the tribesman makes his ceremonial bond with his chief, the subject swears his oath to support his king. In Britain, loyalty retains this personal characteristic, so West can appropriately assume that treason is an offense to basic human relations. In doing so, however, she proceeds from a premise that politically must be qualified in much of Europe and the world. In the westen and northern rim of Europe one can find hereditary monarchs, but not elsewhere in Europe, and most importantly, not in that area which was causing Europe's political paroxysms. In most of these countries which had abolished their monarchies, the basis of authority had been transferred to a written document, a set of precepts that transcended any particular individual. In this transfer one's loyalty assumes a different nature. Allegiance to one's king need not rely on rational argument; the acceptance of the validity of a set of ideas does. An oath to a sovereign holds one's loyalty differently than does an affirmation of one's allegiance to a state where basic tenets are set forth in its constitution. For West, the traitor, then, is one who has betrayed those closest to him. Whatever reasons he may have for his act of betrayal, those reasons cannot adequately disguise or compensate for this basic disloyalty. With this principle firmly in mind, she could let her search for the traitor's justification for what he has done carry her imaginatively where it would.

Like her, other British writers attempted to understand and make some moral judgment of the traitors among them. It would have been surprising if they had not, for those traitors had been with them for a long time, incipiently as an abrasive, vulgarizing phenomenon that appeared in the public halls and streets before the war, an irritating, sometimes seductive, demoralizing voice that penetrated during the war into the blacked-out privacy of their homes, and after the war as a series of publicized revelations that emerged in the law courts and the newspapers, but through it all these traitors were a reminder that new, powerful forces abroad in the world were at work effecting a diminishment of British prestige and dominion.

Novelists like Elizabeth Bowen and C. P. Snow chose the imaginative route of fiction to explore their understanding of the traitor. Both of them express a sense of puzzlement and outrage at the realization that native Britains, "one of our own," could be capable of an act of betrayal, that he could think and act as a traitor behind a mask of innocence. When he is discovered, his associates ask in disbelief:

"Is he English?"
"As English as I am?"
"I can't understand it."
"I don't want to set up as better than anyone else, and I can understand most things at a push. . . ."
"But as for giving away your country, I can't understand it."
"I could have done the other things, but I couldn't have done that."[13]

For them it was simply a question of personal integrity; they could not accept the "monstrosity of breaking one's oath."[14]

In his book *The Traitors* (1952) the British journalist Alan Moorehead argued that a man's conscience is an unreliable and dangerous governor for his actions, a view that seems limited and excessively partisan when set beside the larger, more eclectic interests of Rebecca West. But this does not necessarily make it less British, for when one views his thesis from the vantage point of the American tradition, a tradition that has celebrated the integrity and rightness of the individual conscience, charac- terized by George Washington as "that little spark of celestial fire,"[15] one can conclude that Moorehead is, like West, expressing a British assumption, an assumption made possible by evolution, not revolution, by stability and tradition, not rapid change, by communal, not individual, aspirations.

To clarify further this British view held by Rebecca West, one can compare it to American responses to treason and also to a study of this same topic by a German writer. The response in the United States to the discovery of treason was violent and divisive. Central to that response were certain constitutional rights that guaranteed individual freedoms. Central also was the controversy as to whether one could be guilty of thinking treasonous thoughts as well as of doing treasonous acts. Loyalty oaths characterized by negations ("I am not and never have been. . . .") were required of innocent and suspect alike and indiscriminately demanded from heterogeneous categories of citizens. To associate with could be as hazardous as being, and no one seemed immune from suspicion. Political fortunes rose and fell on this single issue of treason. The literature generated by it ranges from far-right accusations of worldwide conspiracy to far-left support for the current Communist party line. It was a literature of ideologies, and people became pawns caught up in and often sacrificed to the conflict of those ideologies. Alan Barth's *The Loyalty of Free Men* (1951) was a call to reason in the midst of this hysteria. It is typically American in its reaffirmation of basic American freedoms, but to have felt it was necessary to defend these freedoms is evidence of that American need to reaffirm what the British, even in the midst of spy trials and defections and high government scandals, seem to have taken for granted.

Margret Boveri's *Treason in the Twentieth Century* (1961) is, in its examination of political situations, far more complex than any examination of treason listed here so far. From her vantage point in Germany, Boveri saw how men reacted to political changes that could make right seem wrong and change an effort to achieve an uneasy median between extremes into the appearance of treason. In the world Margret Boveri describes, Alan Moorehead's condemnation of individual conscience seems insupportable because the political chaos of continental Europe caused by World War II compelled individuals caught in this chaos to turn back within themselves and seek there, in their consciences, the moral values that could sustain and motivate them.

Like Rebecca West, Boveri values the perspective that history can contribute. She has lived through enough political change to recognize the truth in Tallyrand's remark, "La trahison—c'est une question du temps," which cynically could be translated as, "Treason—it's a question of recognizing the winning side." Seeking a broader perspective than the contemporary political situation, she found the men she studied, men as different as Knut Hamsun, Marshall Petain, Admiral Darlan, Count von Stauffenberg, Admiral Canaris, Ezra Pound, in surprising agreement with each other in their opposition to what she describes as "the Holy Trinity of capitalism, bourgeoisie and natural science."[16] These men hated the power of money in daily life; they hated the suppression of individuality in factory and office; they were skeptical about parliamentary democracy, and they did not believe in "progress" and the absolute sovereignty of common sense and reason. They were men either opposed to or in uneasy relationship with fascism, which had drawn its followers from what West characterized as "the mindless, traditionless, possessionless urban populations that are the children of the machine."[17] Boveri quotes the theory of Eugen Rosenstock-Huessy that "the appearance of a special sort of deceitful person is the necessary preliminary and accompanying symptom of all great revolutionary changes in the life of politics"[18] as prelude to her observation that "today we live in just such an era, an era of discord, division, and duplicity."[19] The historical perspective of Europe that Boveri describes here is one to which West could respond. And, likewise, when West comments that "treason is inherent in fascism,"[20] Boveri would have been alert to the possibility that the statement could cut two ways. Two perceptive observers of what in the third and fourth decades of this century were the opposing centers of political opinion seem here to arrive at similar conclusions, though the evidence of treason they examined is strikingly different.

IV   The Meaning of Treason: *First Edition*

The books West published on treason are mainly a series of editions that began as *The Meaning of Treason* (1947) and concluded as *The New Meaning of Treason* (1964). These editions are altered by the author as new material became available to her. As she absorbed this additional material, which

consisted primarily of the cases of the Communist traitors, she
changed and deleted some of the old material on the Nazi
traitors. The final result was a balanced presentation of the two
groups of traitors.

The first edition of Rebecca West's *The Meaning of Treason*
appeared first in New York, not in London. The British edition
appeared over a year later than the New York edition. Its
contents are the same. In these first editions West combined
essays she had written for the *New Yorker* on the two most
important defectors to Germany, William Joyce and John Amery,
with the essay on treason written for *Harper's*, and added a new
section on the less important traitors. The first part of the
Harper's essay was deleted, including the reference to the left-
wing writers who had been critical of nationalism. A note and an
epigraph were added at the beginning of the book, the note
explaining how much of the book's material was obtained and
that fictitious names were used for some of the minor traitors,
the epigraph, a quotation from Acts (1:17–20), describing how
one who "was numbered among us" was destroyed because for
money he had exchanged his hope for salvation. The perfidy
characteristic of the traitor sets the tone of the book.

The divisions of her book characterize her interpretation of
the motives of the traitors. The first section, entitled "The
Revolutionary," which comprises two-thirds of the book, she
devoted to one traitor, William Joyce. By far the most significant
of the defectors to Germany, he seems a mass of contradictions
and inconsistencies. He was born in the United States of Irish
parents. When they returned to Ireland he sided with the British
in their struggle against the Sinn Fein revolutionaries. A poor
man, he admired the British aristocracy inordinately and tried to
imitate it, but, though an expert horseman, he still could not
demonstrate even this gentlemanly accomplishment without
being recognized by one who was born to that class as not
belonging. When young he aspired to a military career. Denied
that, he promptly joined the British Fascists. More successful
than most men at stimulating drastic action, he remained fated,
West was convinced, to be passed over for any preferment his
efforts should have assured him. Of an unprepossessing physical
appearance, he had a voice that could magnetize a crowd, and
became so much a part of the British wartime experience that
when he was a fugitive after the war one short sentence he

uttered betrayed his identity. He felt a profound devotion to the old England, but could gloat publicly over Germany's destruction of it by aerial bombardment. A proud man conscious of his abilities and yearning for respect, he earned only the opprobrious title, Lord Haw Haw, by which he will be remembered in history.

The revolutionary, as West described him, is composed also of contradictions that she concentrated into one statement:

. . .a revolutionary blows both hot and cold: he hates order and he loves it. He wants to overthrow the order which exists and which may be the only order capable of existing. But he risks the annihilation of all order only because he believes he can evade that disaster and can substitute for the existing order another which he believes to be superior.[21]

The revolutionary, if successful, causes an event that too is contradictory, "a vast explosion of the creative powers, and nothing is created; nothing is even altered,"[22] or, as West characterized the French Revolution, "afterwards proved never to have happened."[23] But on William Joyce the lessons of history were lost; he was too preoccupied in working out his own revolutionary destiny to learn from them.

West puzzles long and hard over Joyce's motivations. She examines his legitimate claim to American citizenship from as many vantage points as she can conceive, but she never explains to her satisfaction why Joyce's father would have obscured this fact and Joyce himself would have denied it by word and act. She suggests that his commitment to revolution is an evidence of his psychological immaturity, that his repudiation of his parents' religion and way of life anticipated a comparable repudiation of his first wife and of the England for which as a child he claimed to have endangered his life: all of these revulsions evidencing his basic incapacity to say "Yes" to what he has. She understands the agony of the soul that living in an Ireland tortured by fractured loyalties could create, but realizes as well that others have had the same experiences and still have emerged capable of more positive purpose than he. She recognizes his considerable intellectual gifts, his ability to inform, to charm, to persuade, and even to secure from some an abiding devotion, but puts in the balance beside them his coarseness, his urge to hurt others, to

dominate, to embrace absolutist solutions. She recognizes him as
a Fascist, but not one of the traditional types. He was not a
flawed example of the aristocracy with a compulsion to dominate
as was Sir Oswald Mosley. Nor was he a soldier, like Franco, who
moved through that profession to political power, abandoning as
he did so the self-abnegation that would have kept him in proper
balance with the society he served. Joyce was of a third type new
to the twentieth century, the Fascist who rises from the lower
classes. Still, the flaw in Joyce prevented his achieving that
public acceptance and admiration he sought. What he did have
that was denied to his fellow traitors was "the chance to wrestle
with reality, to argue with the universe, to defend the revelations
which [he] believed had been made to [his] spirit. . . ."[24]

The second section of *The Meaning of Treason* West entitled
"The Insane Root." Here the traitors she examined are John
Amery and Norman Baillie-Stewart. Both of them she labels
psychotics, a term she defines as the condition of being at war,
not with one's self, but with one's environment. If their psychoses
are related to politics, such men are by their nature easily
persuaded to commit treason. But neither of these two men
seems to have been basically motivated by politics or even by the
desire for great power. The devils that tempted John Amery had
their origins in his desire to enjoy life spiced by danger and
reckless pleasure without having to pay the tab. He was a
confidence man until his family, distinguished and respected, was
forced to declare him bankrupt. Banished to the Continent, he
sought quick profits from Franco's forces in the Spanish Civil
War as earlier he had done from the vulnerable element of the
business community in England. From then on he could not keep
politics and the pleasures of life separate; politics provided the
wherewithal that made the pleasures possible, and the rising
level of general anarchy made it all somehow more acceptable.

The psychosis of Norman Baillie-Stewart seems simpler to
West: a sexual fascination for German women conditioned by a
querulous, dour unwillingness to accept the incongruities of life.
If John Amery could be thought of as the man who invited
himself to dinner, Norman Baillie-Stewart was the man who got
dressed for dinner but whom no one took seriously enough to
invite. As West describes his history, he provided the English
public with some good laughs, German intelligence agents with
some cat-and-mouse games, and German bureaucracy with an

opportunity to show that it too could make errors, but through it all he seems to have understood little of what was happening to him. The ironic humiliation of his trial after World War II was that, though the judge recommended he be sent back to Germany, authorities in Germany would not accept him.

Neither of these men created a threat equal to William Joyce, perhaps because their flaws appeared in the small, often repeated incidents of their lives. West felt some admiration for Joyce; for Amery and Baillie-Stewart she felt something more akin to pity and contempt. In their aberrant behavior they help support her thesis that when a nation lets power entice it into irrational acts, then those individuals who have an insecure grip on reality will find their way to treason.

The third section of *The Meaning of Treason*, entitled "The Children," is the record of those innocents who, because of fear and inexperience and perhaps some inherent flaw of character, could not withstand the pressures to which their enemies subjected them. They were corrupted and used and finally discarded as the other traitors were not. Norman Baillie-Stewart was fated to be suspect and neglected, yet even his experience is preferable to that of the "children," those naive adolescents who were subjected to cruelties and vulgarities the other traitors did not know. One of them, only fourteen years of age when he was captured by the Germans, was coerced into the British Free Corps, that group of turncoats whose purpose was to fight on the Russian front. Having the distinction of being the only private in the corps, he was abandoned for many months, then sent east when that front was collapsing, captured by the Russians, and finally returned to the British. The other "children" were used as espionage agents in the prisoner-of-war camps. Loneliness dominated their lives, loneliness punctuated by taunts and threats, conditioned by fear and shame. They knew they had done wrong. Their sense of guilt came in a simple form from that same source West finds typical of all traitors; they had betrayed those closest to them, the protectors of their childhood. The real villains were those who frightened and enticed and corrupted these children, villains like John Amery who exploited them for his own corrupt purposes. When Amery was found guilty, West records how the judge, old in years and close to his own death, expressed accusatory puzzlement as he said, "They called you traitor and you heard them."[25] Even this old man who had faced

human perfidy so often found base treason beyond his com-
prehension.

It is in her perceptive reporting of moments like this that one
of the significant excellences of her book can be found. Certainly
the characters deserve the care she uses in portraying them, but
that she can succeed so well is dependent in large part on the
fact that they are caught for us in one of the climactic moments
of their lives, this confrontation in a courtroom where first they
are stripped to a starkness difficult otherwise to achieve, and
then they are judged. One of West's excellences as a reporter is
to make these events pulse with excitement. They read like good
fiction, which is to say that they convey to the reader a sentient,
believable world in which people live and respond to each other
within a complex system laden with tradition and symbols and
expressive of a significant social order. Not one to ignore an
opportunity to penetrate to the meaning of an object or an act
obscured by arcane professionalism or dulled by usage or
neglect, West finds here adequate stimulation for her inquiring
mind. Little escapes her attention, not the legal intricacies
related to Joyce's citizenship and his use of a British passport, not
the ceremony of Joyce's trial before the House of Lords, not the
inept inexperience of the officers who conducted the court-
martial of that pitiful traitor Stoker Rose, not the historical irony
that the trial of another traitor, John Welch, was held in the room
of a great house where Ribbentrop had been warmly entertained
by British aristocracy, not even the fruity word game—Herr
Obst, Fraulein Marie Louise, Alphonse Poiret—some German
agents played on Baillie-Stewart, a man too unimaginative to
respond to the game.

The first edition of *The Meaning of Treason* is satisfying in its
completeness. It creates an understandable order out of the
zealots, the opportunists, the maladjusted, and the unfortunates
who had deserted Britain for Germany in World War II. And yet
this edition is only the prelude to a succession of refinements and
additions that become the process by which West arrives at her
final statement on treason. The clue to the book's possible
tentativeness is present in it. By the time it appeared the first of
the Communist traitors, Alan Nunn May, had been detected and
tried. West tried to assimilate him into her gallery of traitors, but
in that company he remains an anomaly. He is not of the same
order, not in his allegiance, his training, his method, his sense of

purpose. His cause was in the ascendance, the cause of Joyce and the others of his persuasion was lost.

V   The Meaning of Treason: *Revisions and Additions*

The second British edition of *The Meaning of Treason* (1952) begins the process of revision and addition by which West produced eventually *The New Meaning of Treason*. One small but significant change she made was to drop the poet Roy Campbell from her list of members in the British Union of Fascists. In a letter to the *Times Literary Supplement* (December 23, 1949) she apologized for including him in the list and stated that she would remove mention of him from future editions. The most important addition was a section entitled "The New Phase." This title indicates that the author realized her previous categorizations—"The Revolutionary," "The Insane Root," "The Children"—would no longer suffice. The significance of this new traitor lies more in what he did than what he was. It was a "New Phase": in its chronology, in its identification of a new enemy, in the education and social status of its traitors, in its reliance on espionage rather than propaganda. With a preliminary caveat to the long list of traitors who have had a role to play throughout history in the making and undoing of civilizations, West uses much of this new section of the book to describe those aspects of modern Britain that, in her view, induced an atmosphere congenial to the development of this new kind of traitor, the scientist-intellectual, who had his roots in the middle class and had exceptional, highly trained, mental capabilities. The general impetus for this traitor came from his dissatisfaction and disillusionment with capitalistic industrial society. The source of this discontent he felt originated in two groups: the industrial workers themselves and a more heterogeneous group of individuals of all classes who, for humanitarian reasons, were revolted by the insensitive cruelties they saw as a characteristic of the industrial system. These groups found their most articulate spokesmen in Sidney and Beatrice Webb, who attempted through their creation, the Fabian Society, to reform society as they knew it. The connection that reached from these earnest, well-meaning reformers to the scientist-traitors is one more of temperament and attitude than of cumulative developments.

The faith that inspired [the generation of the Webbs] to rebellion was socialism, and since that is now the established practice of [the] land [their children] must find another dissident faith. . . . It is on the Left, where they learned in their infancy salvation lay.[26]

Communism was the one possibility left.

A scientist with this political bias could add to it the grievance that he, the advocate of reason, the master of Nature's secrets, the benefactor of modern civilization, had not been rewarded adequately by that society. He looked about him at the social and political world he inhabited and felt assured that with his superior abilities he could do better. At least he knew best what should be done with his own creations. In terms of sheer power nothing surpassed the knowledge possessed by the scientists who had developed the atomic bomb during World War II. If they could create such power, did they not have the wisdom and the responsibility to determine how that power should be used? This question they must have asked themselves. At least some did, and those who belong in West's book answered in the affirmative and then acted to disperse and, as they thought, neutralize knowledge by conveying it to the Communists, the advocates of that political system they saw as the hope of the future.

The picture of Communist treason West creates includes primarily one portrait, that of Klaus Fuchs, and a sketch of Alan Nunn May. Alan Nunn May exemplifies the kind of traitor— earnest, committed, drably austere—West can explain with her description of the British reform movement. Klaus Fuchs cannot be so explained, for he is the result of almost the obverse situation, the chaos and fractured loyalties of post-World War I Germany. The son of a pastor who opposed Hitler for religious and pacifistic reasons long after it was dangerous to do so, Klaus Fuchs was active politically even as a student. As West expressed it, he was "involved in the useless and silly and violent political activities by which German undergraduates have done so much to destroy the civil order and social coherence of their country."[27] While still a student he joined the Communist Party, went into hiding when the Reichstag fire signaled the triumph of Hitler, and then was helped by the Communist party to leave Germany. Within a short time he appeared in England, where he was given aid to study at British universities. He was deported to Canada as an alien early in World War II, and then permitted to return to England to continue his research and eventually to work on the atomic project both in Britain and in the United States. Only shortly before he was arrested did he express any concern for the consequences his treasonous actions would have on his associates. Like Alan Nunn May he had made his commitment early and had followed it without deviation. Like May he exemplified, to use West's term, "the infantilist; and since it is perfectly possible for a highly gifted intellectual to be an infantilist, it appeared not surprising that a prominent English scientist should be a Communist, and therefore, since every Communist is bound to regard treachery as one of his Party duties, a traitor."[28] This is a harsh judgment, but it seems fair enough for these two men, especially if one recalls the "Cold War" atmosphere in which it was made.

In 1956 West revised *The Meaning of Treason* again, this time for Pan Books Limited. In her "Foreword" she describes how she began her investigation of treason and how, with the trial of Alan Nunn May, she realized that the historical event she was observing had passed into a second phase. The difference in the public response to William Joyce and Alan Nunn May—repudiation of Joyce, sympathy for May—convinced her that the task she had set for herself was not just to describe, but also to persuade. The public was willing to see May as a traitor, but it was not willing to conceive of him as anything more than an amateur spy. In contrast, West judged him more severely than she did William Joyce: Joyce was the amateur, May was "an ice-cold professional, at home in our age."[29] She intimates that the propaganda resources of the Communist Party may have abetted this milder public reaction. West began her study of treason because she thought it necessary to supply the public with information it did not have; now she felt compelled to protect it from "misinformation that was being given it with both hands."[30] These alterations of situation and attitude prepare us for a hardening in her attitude towards traitors. These men, she concludes, not only undermine the state, they corrupt it; they not only betray other men, they force them to act as they themselves do.

In the Pan edition West includes her account of the defection of the last important British scientist-traitor, Bruno Pontecorvo, plus those officials from the British Foreign Office, Donald Maclean and Guy Burgess, who, when their espionage activities

were discovered, escaped, like Pontecorvo, behind the Iron
Curtain in a smudge of publicity. To accommodate this new
material West telescoped two sections from the earlier editions,
"The Insane Root" and "The Children," into a new section
entitled "In Need of Care and Protection" and enlarged the
section "The New Phase" to include all the added material. She
also dropped the "Epilogue," which was based on the *Harper's*
essay "The Meaning of Treason" and had been a feature of all
previous editions, and added her summary remarks to the end of
"The New Phase."

Previously in her summary she had described why treason was
an act inimical to civilization, but she had not attempted to assess
personal blame. If she had tried to make this kind of assessment
in her book, she did so as an immediate consequence of analyzing
a particular instance of treason: the Irish situation as it related to
William Joyce, the Fabian Society as it contributed to the
attitudes of Alan Nunn May, Germany of the 1920s and Klaus
Fuchs, but it was in the main body of the book, not in the
epilogue. Seeking a fitting conclusion to this new edition, she
returned to her thesis that significant forces in society can
stimulate attitudes in individuals. Such a thesis has its dangers,
particularly when associated with individuals still alive; she had
had one rebuff already when she named Roy Campbell as a
member of the British Union of Fascists.

In the Pan edition, West worked out her conclusion by
comparing the patriotic bravery of Lieutenant Terence Waters,
a prisoner of war in Korea, with the treachery of Alan Nunn May.
When Lieutenant Waters realized that he and his men faced
certain death in the prison camp, he ordered his men to join a
turncoat group called "Peace Fighters." He saved the lives of his
men, but he stayed in the camp and died there. The actions of
both Lieutenant Waters and Alan Nunn May were calculated,
astute, and successful, yet, West observes, many English people
would feel more comfortable with May than with Waters. Asking
why this was so, she cited what for her was evidence in modern
imaginative literature, using as illustrations the work of Evelyn
Waugh and Graham Greene. The consequences of this accusa-
tion have been described already. But, remembering her motive
for publicizing treason and her dedication that carried her
through years of effort, these consequences, however just, seem
ironic. Her intent was moral in emphasis; she felt too many of her

contemporaries had lost those values that motivated Lieutenant Waters and had substituted for them a decadent aesthetics that could glamorize the world of the professional spy. The morality of the spy she cannot accept. "It is a matter of fundamental preference: loyalty loves life and treachery hates it."[31] So she is led to make such an adverse, highly charged judgment.

VI   The New Meaning of Treason

In 1964, eight years after the Pan edition, West published *The New Meaning of Treason,* her final version of her study of traitors. In the intervening years a new group of traitors, all of them spies, had been uncovered and tried. To accommodate this new material she again revised the structure of her book, dropping the section entitled "In Need of Care and Protection" but retaining "The Revolutionary" and "The New Phase," and adding to them a third section, "Decline and Fall of Treason," plus a new "Conclusion." With this new format she completes her process of revision. Her initial concept was based on the types of traitors she encountered, here her model is history. It should be added that in this version, as in those preceding, West was not simply rearranging parts. Her revisions extended into the text, reflecting her changing concept of her audience, or her new perception of her topic, or simply her sense of style. For what they reveal of how an author can fashion and refine, these versions provide an example deserving of more minute study than can be provided here.

By the time West prepared this last version, she felt assured that the process that began with the efforts to complete the unfinished business of World War II among the ruins and austerities of postwar Britain, that moved through the growing awareness of how the Soviet Union had fostered a new breed of committed, professional spies, and that deteriorated finally into apolitical scandals characterized by greed and lechery, had reached its end. She had a grudging respect for William Joyce, less for Fuchs and May, but only revulsion for Vassall and the other traitors of this last phase. West was willing to weigh and assess more carefully in the early cases. Later, as if she had seen the pattern repeated too often, or she had clarified the issues beyond debate in her own mind, or she simply found these traitors less worthy of her attention, she became less willing to entertain the rationales they gave for their actions. She was more apt to judge them on the basis of one essential question: did they commit treason?

Her primary target in the new section of her book is the professionlism that characterized most of the spies of this last phase. This professionalism took various forms. It could be the ability to blend chameleonlike into the necessary situation. Or it could be based on some special expertise, like photography or electronics. Or it could find expression in the satisfaction of doing a good job and being paid for it without any commitment to a particular political ideology. This professionalism could mean simply accepting the risks of that job, learning what to do if caught, and dismissing any moral qualms as irrelevant. It could even find expression in the desire that others think well of the profession itself. This professionalism indicated to West how far treason had come in being accepted by modern nations as an institutionalized element necessary to their existence. This necessity she recognized but abhorred.

The nature of these traitors can be seen in their ability to blend into the institutions they serve. If they occupy government positions, they are, like Harry Houghton and Winifred Gee, functionaries, not policymakers. They have access to records, but do not create these records. If they work their trade in other ways, they are, like Stephen Ward of the Profumo case, purveyors on the fringes of power; they satisfy human needs and exploit human weaknesses. All of them are evidence of how in the twentieth century people in low positions can influence great public events. The size and complexity of modern institutions require great numbers of functionaries to make them work and great masses of records to ensure adequate exchange of information. Security never seems foolproof, so the potential is there for anyone with access to these records and an eye to their importance to use them for subversive purposes. There is nothing new about stealing state secrets, but the methods have changed, the opportunities have increased.

As one example of how these traitors functioned, the case of John Vassall can be cited. West explores it thoroughly. In the United States it is not so well known as the scandal caused by Mr. Profumo's relation with Christine Keeler, but in Britain it was highly publicized and eventually involved several branches of government, members of Parliament, and the press. West prepared a special report of it, entitled *The Vassall Affair*, which was published by the *Sunday Telegraph*. Later she reduced that book into the account she gives in *The New Meaning of Treason*.

John Vassall worked as a clerk in various government offices. He began his activities as a spy when he, like another spy, William Marshall, was sent to the British embassy at Moscow, where he, again like Marshall, was solicited for espionage activities. When he returned to Britain he established a routine of removing documents, photographing them—a skill he had learned in the RAF—and then returning them before their absence was detected. This activity he continued over a period of eight years and was paid well for it. If left at this, his case is comparatively simple. But he was a homosexual, and when his spying was discovered the question was asked: Why was security so lax? Interest again was promoted and others fell under suspicion. It was a scandal that seemed to proliferate tentacles like an octopus. When finally the facts were sorted out, the hysteria waned, the innocents affirmed, and blame assessed, as much damage had been done to the public's confidence in its government as John Vassall had done in his years of selling photographs of documents, which amounted to a hefty, unexpected dividend to the Soviet Union.

West concludes that the problem of an espionage case like this is the consequence of several factors. They can be summarized as the unmanageability of overwhelming numbers, the incongruity of secret agencies in an open society, and the old human impulse to derive advantage and pleasure from the misfortune of someone else. She sees little possibility of preserving sweet order in the midst of such roiling forces of contradictory impulse. West ends *The New Meaning of Treason* by repeating in a variety of ways the same exhortation: Let us learn from what we have experienced. Some specific corrections the government had made already, as evidenced by its amending the military court-martial procedures. But most of the lessons were more general. Let history teach us what it can. Be wary of those human characteristics that the examples in this book show us are prone to treachery. Don't let sentimentality cloud our awareness that the traitor is "a thief and a liar,"[32] and that "treachery is a sordid and undignified form of crime."[33] Remember that loyalty can effectively counter treason. Most important, be sure to keep that essential balance between national security and individual liberties, without which none of the rest is of value.

West's twenty-year study of treason is the most accessible record she has left of how she can grow intellectually in a subject. Her general view of human nature is not different from that presented in *Black Lamb and Grey Falcon* or *The Court and the Castle,* but her awareness of how man accommodates to the particular baseness of treason increases from case to case until she can look at the complex and see the simple, and then write of what is and what should be. She demonstrates here in a unique fashion that informing purpose of much that she has written, the urge for self-enlightenment through the clarifying process of the created work. As she has stated in another context, the book becomes experience.

VII   A Train of Powder

Rebecca West wrote a companion study to *The Meaning of Treason.* This book, *A Train of Powder* (1955), also is based on court trials, and it too has its origins in the period of relief and disorder and aspiration for a new moral order that followed the end of World War II. The book contains six essays. Three of the essays are based on her reports of the Nuremberg trials and their aftermath. Interstices among these essays are the accounts of three other trials: one caused by a lynching in South Carolina, a second the result of a gang-type murder in London, a third the conclusion of one of the more curious cases of treason. West wrote these accounts for periodicals and later assembled them here. The title she chose, *A Train of Powder,* is from Sermon 26 by John Donne. The appropriate passage, expressing the omnipotent power of God, is used as an epigraph in the book: "Our God is not out of breath, because he hath blown one tempest, and swallowed a Navy: our God hath not burnt out his eyes, because he hath looked upon a Train of Powder."[34] Perhaps even more pertinent to the subject of her book is the sentence that follows this passage, expressing more the omniscience of God than his omnipotence: "In the light of Heaven, and in the darkness of Hell, he sees alike."[35] West's book is about judgments, how difficult they are to make and how problemati- cal as justice, so her title could be read as a caution that when we attempt to judge the men on trial in this book, we and they are the objects of a more equable vision.

West begins her book with her report on the Nuremberg trials. Her theme at first is boredom, boredom plus cyclamens. The tension between the prisoners who dread a conclusion to the trial and the others who see that conclusion as their release from the purgatorial limbo in which they presently find themselves stretches everyone on this rack of strained boredom. The cyclamens which give the essay its title are in their rich elegance an anomaly in this scene where so much is lacking and death in word and appearance is a haunting presence. West found them one day in the greenhouse at the villa where she and other journalists were billeted. A perfection of its kind, the greenhouse was kept by those ill adapted to care for it, a one-legged man and a child of twelve. The incongruities she sees here she finds everywhere else, piling one on another, ultimately forming a grotesque horror that robs almost everyone of grace or compassion. Everything—the people, their actions and speech, the architecture, the trial itself—is misshapen and excessive. What laughter there is is derisive. The evidences she sees of love appear to be fugitive and basically selfish. Hatred is dominant, so also is condescension. The description West gives us lacks neutrality; it is the effect on her of a holocaust lapsing finally into the emotions swirling in that courtroom. We are told at the beginning of the essay that the plane carrying her to Nuremberg is descending into the midst of the world's enemy, and we note that the year is 1946, which accounts for much that is in the essay. It should be noted too that nine years earlier West had reacted just as sharply to whatever was Germanic in Yugoslavia and had opened and closed her history of that country with descriptions of ominous intrusions of Germans into it. The war had intervened and now she could write a conclusion to what she had dreaded nine years earlier. The prisoners at Nuremberg had for too many years loomed fearfully large; seeing them as diminished figures in the dock, she could reduce them to the inconsequents she would have preferred them to be. But some distinction in her response between the Nazi regime and the German people, as was made for example in Abby Mann's *Judgment at Nuremberg*, would have lifted a little the pall of malaise and contempt described here.

The other two essays on Germany describe the transition of that country from defeat and ruin to prosperity. The traits West found in the one-legged nurseryman are used to explain both

Germany's miraculous recovery and its potential for future disaster. The second essay does mitigate the harshness of the first essay, but not too much, because West cannot forget the cyclamen grower who, to her thinking, is not someone who loves to grow beautiful flowers, but instead is a potter of plants, one who feels only "the itch to industry, the lech for work."[36] She sees him as a forerunner of a nation given to pushy, laissez-faire business practices, with an appetite like Gerda's for the rich products of the Konditorei, and a drive to dominate. She does credit West Germany for its success in assimilating the refugees from East Europe, thereby lifting a moral weight from the Allies. She supports even stronger the stand of the Berliners during the Blockade. Their courage precipitated what she saw as a dialogue between two ideologies which would end, she hoped, in the establishment of truth. But these are only glimmerings through the general dour censure.

The third essay returns to the subject of the Nuremberg trials, but this time through the medium of a book she is reading while attending a conference of economists in 1954 in Switzerland. The book is written by a man who was acquitted at Nuremberg. The conference of economists includes Germans who demonstrate a prosperity equal to that of anyone at the conference. She sets what she sees as the book's self-serving argument that the trial had not achieved what the Allies had intended beside her impression of the German economists "who bustled in with the air, modest yet consequential, of not being the performers but of being essential to the performance,"[37] and concludes that the man in the greenhouse, the representative man of West Germany, had not learned "the lesson Berlin might have taught him."[38] Her response is still negative, but she has muted the tone in which she states it.

The other three essays in the book are a disparate group. In one of them the author presents the trial of the traitor William Marshall, an account she later incorporates into *The New Meaning of Treason*. The remaining two essays present murder trials, one of a lynching in the American South, the other of a murder for profit in London. There is not much in common between these murders. The lynching was the result of a caste system that excited strange impulses in men; a black man would hire a taxi because by that means he could make a white man work for him, but the aberration led to a murder and a lynching and a trial with no convictions. The other murder was produced by the stresses caused by postwar shortages which greedy men exploited to satisfy the desires of other greedy men. Both essays help West illustrate how strange and sinister the workings of the human mind often are. Justice on this earth is not perfect, not in Nuremberg, or in Greenville, South Carolina, or in London; but neither the enormity of a crime, nor the prejudice that makes it appear not to be a crime, nor the concealment of that crime can pass by unobserved by an all-seeing God.

In a general sense the principal characters of this book do belong with West's gallery of traitors. Their self-serving actions are expressive of their capacity for self-delusion. They, like the traitors, descend into a nether world where they exchange the well-ordered life for strange, dyspeptic, often savage satisfactions that in the end do not satisfy. Also like the traitors, they will always be with us. So when we come to the conclusion of *A Train of Powder,* we are not presented with answers or solutions, only with possibilities. Taken in balance, West's exploration of these dark corners of the human spirit does provide us with charts that in their immediate detail are clear enough, but remain only segments of something larger in which the interrelations of this part to that are left too indeterminate.

CHAPTER 5

Novelist: Early Experiments

REBECCA West's career as a novelist extends over most of her mature life. Her first novel, *The Return of the Soldier*, appeared in 1918 when she was twenty-six years old. Her latest novel, *The Birds Fall Down*, appeared in 1966 when she was seventy-four. In all she has published seven novels, plus a book of short novels and some short, fugitive fiction in each of these six decades except the 1940s, so her interest and effort have been continuous.

As a journalist West prides herself on her professional efficiency. She has a quick, alert mind that can absorb, organize, and state a complex series of facts with remarkable speed. It is improbable, though, that as a novelist she would wish to be known by the same characteristics. Her novels do not read as if they were prepared that way. They are too intricate, too stylized, too constructed.

For her, writing fiction is the culmination rather than the initial or intermediary phase of an interest she may have. As one reads through Rebecca West's publications one discovers that her interests, like those of most of us, surge and ebb. If there is a difference, it would be that her interests drive her more intensely than they do most of us. When she finds a new topic her first literary expression of it is descriptive and expository—journalistic, if you will, but exhibiting evidence of a process of assimilation. The second phase shows her attempting to synthesize, to draw general conclusions, to search for first principles, to put this new interest in the context of other interests she may have. In the process so far, the author constantly keeps her attention on the reality she is observing, but at this point West lets the topic lie in her mind until her imagination activates a fictive form it can assume. So her novels are conceived. West wrote many essays about feminism and then followed them with two novels weighted with feminist interests. Her years as a

130

literary critic found fictive expression in *Harriet Hume.* Her concern about European political developments in the 1930s led her to write *The Thinking Reed.* She followed twenty years of writing about treason with her novel *The Birds Fall Down.* Observation and rational analysis have in each case led to imaginative, fictive synthesis.

But though we recognize this process, we cannot assume that it finds its best expression in its final form. Rebecca West's literary genius is not basically fictive. She has a wonderfully observant eye and a remarkable ability to recreate in words what she has observed. She delights in working with concepts and has a gift for persuasive argument. It is this delight and this gift that serve as the matrix for the observed detail in most of her writing, not the narrative urge of the storyteller. The impulse of her young Suffragette heroine in *The Judge* to spend much of her time mentally composing persuasive speeches she is too shy to deliver seems an authentic memory of the author's own youth.

Yet West desires to tell stories. It is, though, a desire that is not continuous, all absorbing. One canot conceive of her writing fiction a la George Sand or Anthony Trollope, thirty pages a day, year after year. One can conceive of her sandwiching it in among all the journalistic deadlines she has had to face, or, preferably, seeking those quiet periods in which she could dedicate herself to this more sanctified task. As a journalist she has a profession; as a novelist she desires, one suspects, to be thought of as having a vocation.

Her novels were popular successes. When *The Fountain Overflows* appeared, it was chosen for circulation by the Literary Guild, and *The Birds Fall Down* was a Book-of-the-Month Club selection. Some of the novels, including her first one, *The Return of the Soldier,* have been reprinted recently as paperbacks. Her fiction has been widely read, but it has not won the praise given to other of her books like *Black Lamb and Grey Falcon* and *The New Meaning of Treason.*

I   The Return of the Soldier

Rebecca West's first novel, *The Return of the Soldier,* appeared in 1918. It is a short novel, about 30,000 words. Two years earlier she had published her first book, a critical study of Henry James, and her interest in James's literary techniques lingers on in this novel. It is a story of a soldier, Chris, who, because of shell shock, suffers from a fifteen-year hiatus of memory. It is a story as well of the three women who love him: his wife, Kitty; Margaret, whom he loved as a youth; and his cousin Jenny, whom he has known all his life. Jenny narrates the story, The soldier has wealth, a beautiful estate, and a wife befitting these attributes, but he does not remember her. He remembers Margaret instead, that Margaret who lives intensely in his memory as she was when he knew her. When he is brought home he desires to see her, and even though she is middle-aged, married, and scarred by poverty and hard work, he loves her as he loved her before. The task falls to her to destroy this idyll by forcing him to remember, to return to reality. She goes back to her obscure marriage and he returns to the war.

But he could have returned to almost any activity because, despite its title, *The Return of the Soldier* does not give us any authentic sense of what war is about. As a statement about World War I it lacks the significance Robert Graves, Edmund Blunden, and Seigfried Sassoon gave to their war memoirs. It pales to insignificance beside Vera Brittain's presentation of the war in her novel *Honourable Estate* or her memoir *The Testament of Youth*. For West the war was a negative force that seems to be evoked simply to cause Chris's loss of memory. It was a contemporary convenience to be used by West to create a situation that James would have found attractive. West's interest is in a situation that has its origins not in the war, but in part in an old novelistic convention of the man torn between two concepts of woman, in part in West's own personal experiences.

The novel is built on contrasts, the most striking of which exists between the soldier's wife and the woman he had loved earlier. His wife, Kitty, is self-centered, blond, demanding, and as glittering and unconsciously cruel as the diamonds she wears. Margaret is dowdy in appearance, dark, yet has compassion and understanding. The sentimental novel's convention of the light and dark ladies is still operative here, but the empathetic response they create is pushed to extremes. The corollary to this opposition of women is the division within the soldier himself between his wish to live in the world of idyllic love and his need to return to his real world of social obligation and military duty. A critic as early as Joseph Collins[1] has noted the Freudian characteristics of this situation and recognized the novel as an innovating effort to make Freud's psychoanalytic interests literarily viable. But West's presentation lacks subtlety. She pushes the reader toward an awareness of the psychoanalyst's intrusion by making the novel's climax hinge on the medical cure of the soldier's amnesia. A doctor is introduced and he convinces Margaret to effect his cure, even though she has a better, instinctive understanding of what must be done and why it must be done than does the doctor himself, and she is the only one who can do it.

Admitting that West could have been aware of Freud when she conceived this novel, one should recognize that other influences are at work. The soldier's condition, the splitting of his character into two parts, reflects a fascination with variants of the doppelgänger that in preceding decades had been very much a part of the literary imagination. Stevenson, Wilde, James, and Conrad: all had used it. Stevenson and Wilde were satisfied to present their doubles as compounds of good and evil. James and Conrad presented more psychological states—what might have been, what could be—a complex of the actual and the potential or the desired. West approximates that subtler sense of psychological verities found in James's *The Jolly Corner* and Conrad's *The Secret Sharer*, though her devices for describing the subtleties of the human psyche are cruder and more clinical.

Evident also in *The Return of the Soldier* is an unevenness of presentation. Some pages are rich with observed detail and felt experience. The part of the novel set in a rural retreat, Monkey Island at Bray, has this richness; it is there that Chris and his beloved Margaret spent a wondrous summer of their lost youth. This richness appears elsewhere, usually in association with Margaret. To the extent that Margaret represents what West herself had experienced, the vitality of her presentation is to be expected. Rebecca West knew Monkey Island well; she had spent quiet, peaceful times there with H. G. Wells, and he would have encouraged her to such a response because his memories of it extended back to some of the happiest days of his childhood. So there is a rich feeling in her description of that setting and the memories of love associated with it. Read in this autobiographical context, the soldier's wife, Kitty, is most like H. G. Wells's wife, Jane, but not so much as she actually was as what she would have meant emotionally to Rebecca West, who could lay claim to Wells's love, but not to his social position or his home. Rebecca

West did think Jane Wells was attempting to destroy her relation
with Wells, but she thought Wells contributed to this effort by
his impulse to sacrifice the sexual woman to the nonsexual
woman. In her novel West piles the disadvantages against
Margaret, the sexual woman, so high that she could not succeed
in retaining her lover even if she had so desired.

The feminist interests of this novel lie here in the private
world of the lovers. But West can move no further in her defense
of love as an imperative than did that earlier feminist George
Sand. Both of them accept the validity of love and both insist that
the woman must share in that passion, but both also recognize
that, though *omnia vincit amor* is what they desire, the real
conquerors are society and convention. Love does not conquer
all in post-Victorian England, but it does exist in the sheltered
isolation of Monkey Island at Bray or even in the woods of Baldry
Court, but not in the "black and white magnificence"[2] of Kitty's
bedroom into which, while remodeling the house, she appropri-
ated a small adjacent room Chris had cherished as most
personally his. Acquisitive selfishness, not love, rules here, and its
advocate is one of those parasitic women whom Rebecca West
had attacked in her polemic essays for the *Clarion* in 1912.
British women won their suffrage in 1918, the year this novel was
published, but six years had done little to bring change to the
more difficult and deeply rooted feminist concerns expressed in
this novel.

II   The Judge

Rebecca West's second novel, *The Judge,* appeared in 1922,
four years after *The Return of the Soldier.* It is a longer, much
more ambitious novel, more consistently accomplished in its
presentation of characters. Its structure is carefully planned,
again on a principle of dualities. It has a consistent richness of
observed detail.

The story has three main characters, two of them women. One
is Ellen Melville, young, working at her first job as a secretary
and living with her widowed mother in Edinburgh; the other is
Marion Yaverland, an older woman living on her ancestral farm
in southeast Essex, the mother of two sons, one of them
illegitimate. The illegitimate son, Richard Yaverland, is the link
between these two women. The growth of love between Ellen

and Richard and the death of Ellen's mother constitute the first half of the novel, set in Edinburgh. The second half of the novel opens in Essex, where Richard has taken Ellen to meet his mother. In this context we learn of the mother's history, her love for the local squire, his desertion of her when pregnant, her seeking a desperate refuge in marriage with the squire's butler. After her son Richard is born, the butler forces himself on her and a second son, Roger, who in character is the opposite of his brother, is born. Distraught by years of guilt and remorse, the mother finally commits suicide. Roger's fanatic accusations drive Richard to murder his half-brother. In the last scene Richard and Ellen escape for a short interlude together before he will surrender to the authorities.

The Judge was an achievement excellent enough to capture the attention of contemporary critics like Grant Overton, Joseph Collins, and Patrick Braybrooke. This second novel provided evidence to them that the promise of *The Return of the Soldier* was here amply realized. Grant Overton praised it indiscriminately in *When Winter Comes to Main Street* (1922). Joseph Collins came also to praise, but more judiciously. He is satisfied to classify her as "brilliant," but finds that brilliance best expressed elsewhere than in her novels. Patrick Braybrooke singles out *The Judge* for special praise, but does so while recognizing even here that peculiar liability West has labored under during her entire career, the conflicting desires of the creator and the polemicist; "unless she is careful to keep a check on what she says and writes in the public press, we shall be the spectators of an unfortunate dualism in one woman, a brilliant literary artist and a 'smart' and superficial journalist."[3] Again the word "brilliant," and again a qualification, which the phrase the modern critic Peter Wolfe applied to all her fiction, "a litter of brilliant fragments,"[4] keeps alive still today. Yet of all her novels, *The Judge* was selected for mention in that standard reference, *A Literary History of England.*

If we can rely on the term "brilliant," then we can expect to be caught up by the acute sensibility, the quick observation, the apt language of the author: all are characteristics that appear on page after page of her novel. And we are caught up, even though we do so as we move through this massive novel, with its huge blocks of material and its morbid, sometimes ugly theme. West chose as the epigraph for her novel, "Every mother is a judge who sentences her children for the sins of the father." What but gloom could be generated by a theme that condemns the fathers and requires the mothers to pass judgment on the evidence of the bond that held them together? But if one sees the epigraph as an effort to put a counterweight in the balance that had tipped for so long against the daughters of Eve, it seems, then, though harsh, not so arbitrary as it might at first appear. Present as well in the epigraph is a more general pessimism derived, one would suspect, from that naturalistic matrix of environment and psychology employed by writers like George Gissing, who himself wrote a story entitled "The Sins of the Fathers." One wonders, though, just how much of a sharp twist to the autobiographical Rebecca West intended by dedicating this novel to her mother.

The environment, in the form of the two settings, the city of Edinburgh and the estuary mud-flats of the southeast Essex, is essential to the novel. Though she knew both settings, West does not appear to have used them because she had the kind of emotional attachment for them that Hardy had for Wessex or Bennett had for Staffordshire. Like them, her literary concept of setting is in the general tradition of nineteenth-century novelists like Balzac, who used setting and character as complementary elements supporting each other. To paraphrase Balzac's dictum: *tout son caractère explique ses environs comme ses environs impliquent son caractère.*

Thus Ellen Melville becomes most comprehensible when observed moving through Edinburgh and the countryside about it. Edinburgh is a city of sharp heights and declines. It is dominated by a castle, yet its inhabitants practice a religion that induces sensible independence. It is a city of cold winds, but its inhabitants meet them head on.

[S]uch inclemencies were just part of the asperity of conditions which she reckoned as the price one had to pay for the dignity of living in Edinburgh; . . . since to survive in anything so horrible proved one good rough stuff fit to govern the rest of the world.[5]

The concerns of the spirit did not lapse into softness in Edinburgh; the spirit faced too many challenges. Even conversation had in it the quickness and sharpness of challenge, and Ellen meets the challenge with the best of them.

"You evidently haven't realized that a Scotch girl can't help looking sensible. That graceful butterfly frivolity that comes so easy to the English, and, I've haird, the French, is not for us. I think it's something about our ankles that prevents us."[6]

The preferred attribute of the body in Edinburgh is strength, a kind of upright, virile swagger, best witnessed to the skirling of the bagpipes. Its virtue is bravery, its challenge adventure, but most often circumstances only permit it simply to bide. If the virtue of the body is strength, its temptation is pleasure. Ellen reacts with disgust to her first taste of wine, though she can marvel at its color. The little house in which she and her mother live trembles in the evenings to the pulsating noise of a neighboring dance hall "where ugly people lurched against each other lustfully."[7] For a Scotsman wine is an acquired taste, but dancing is one of his delights, characterized by a light, agile, precise gracefulness that deserves better than the revolting image presented here. Still, this is Edinburgh, where the spirit of John Knox still lowers and the heavy mechanisms of the Industrial Revolution have debauched old customs. Perhaps more to the point is the intrusion of the author's theme, which uses the dance hall to remind Ellen's lover and the reader of all those sinning "men over the world who had committed themselves to that search for pleasure which makes joy inaccessible."[8] Ellen has little time for religion, but here she and Scottish Calvinism are at least proximate to each other. Sex is shameful and secretive and belongs behind closed doors. Ellen feels the injury of it, though she does not understand its motivation, but she is young and unknowing of how utterly her mother "had been violated and crushed by something harsh and reckless."[9]

The life of the intellect is more positive in Edinburgh, the seat of one of Britain's great universities, a center of culture, of religious and political controversy. Ellen's intellectual vitality makes her a true daughter of her city. Our first perception of her is as a Suffragette, a committed and vocal advocate. She had been an excellent student, proud of her achievements and alert to the advantages education can make for a happy and fruitful life. She has the habit of reading and holds strong opinions about what she has read; she can talk of Stevenson and Burns, Barrow and DeQuincey, and for an evening's reading chooses Froude's

Life of Jane Welsh Carlyle. She quotes Latin, knows the art and music that are available to her; she can speak of events from history and has memorized series of facts from the Bible. She responds as willingly to the natural beauty she finds about her; the Pentland Hills are for her an ecstasy: "It was so like her. It was beautiful and solitary even as she was."[10]By the end of Book One, halfway through the novel, the character of Ellen and the setting have become so intimately related that to remove her from it is to wrench her from what has become partly her. Her new destination, Essex, is an alien world.

In Book Two a corresponding relation is created between Marion Yaverland, Richard's mother, and her ancestral home on Kerith Island, where land and sea blend in a primordial richness and meet the overarching weight of the sky as a shimmering level line at the horizon. There are no cliffs, no castle dominating the scene, no quickness of aspiration. A slowness characterizes Marion and the land on which her ancestors have lived for generations. "Here the long preparation of earth's events and their endurance would be evident."[11] The past has left its mark on the folkways and created a sense, stronger than in Edinburgh, of social class; here one's name was important; there, one's wealth. Yet the products of wealth Marion could enjoy while Ellen felt uncomfortable with them. Life was spare and frugal in Scotland; in Essex it can be consumed to a state of surfeit. Marion has an impassive mask that Ellen finds difficult to penetrate, her spirit a heaviness that blunts Ellen's liveliness. She creates silences about her. Yet everything seems more open, more public; windows can be seen through; one can be alone only by escaping into the exposed vastness of the sea marshes.

Unlike Edinburgh, where bodies jostle and bounce off each other, retaining their discreteness, bodies in this estuarial site of primordial life are made to join, to couple, to be part of a larger unity. The consequence, though, has more pain in it than bliss, and the detritus of regeneration lies quick in barnyard and tidal swamp alike. Love, the human expression of this omnipresent process, is as much a hazard to a maiden as it was in Edinburgh, but while Ellen is innocent from ignorance, when Marion was young she had been innocent not in knowledge but in experience. The intellectual energy of Edinburgh and the asperity of its expression is not apparent among these Essex farmers and seamen. Marion reads, but mostly she broods about the past. She tries to do what she thinks is right, but is unable finally to control those instinctual emotions that are so strong in her life.

The contrasts multiply. Setting provides the instrument, and as it is projected in the characters of Ellen and Marion, the possibilities of their coming to an understanding with each other can only diminish into the novel's tragic ending. If this is not enough, Richard, the link between the settings, Ellen's betrothed and Marion's son, lacks strength. He cannot hold it all together. Richard seems two different men in the two settings. In Edinburgh he is successful, powerful, a figure of romance and a man worthy of Ellen. On Kerith Island he loses control. He is so emotionally bound to his mother that Ellen is pushed to the periphery, hardly more than an observer. The change is not believable; he is, in H. G. Wells's term, "a faked hero."[12] Thus that character most essential to holding the author's concept together does not fulfill his task.

Another literary convention can be found here, one that sits at the heart of the sentimental novel. It is surprising to find Rebecca West using it, for if any type of novel should have been anathema to feminists, the sentimental novel and its derivative, the gothic novel, must be it. Though these conventional novels were written for a middle-class feminine audience, they presented women as creatures subject to the tortures and tender worship that men could impose on them. The essential attribute of these women is their chastity. Retaining it they can win what they desire; losing it they must suffer. Marion Yaverland loses her virtue to the conventional sentimental villain, the local squire. The literary convention required that she be punished, so she is stoned through the main street of the village for her transgression and then must go through the torments of a marriage of convenience and the birth of an unwanted second son to atone, however inadequately, for her initial act of love.

From Richardson's Clarissa to Hardy's Tess, literary heroines had suffered and died within this convention. In her novel Rebecca West hardly moves beyond it. She has kept the heroine but has shifted the relationship between mother and son, but the guilt of the original act of love is still there, and it weighs almost as heavily on the son as it does on the mother. Whatever the extent of her emancipation, Rebecca West presents this erotic relationship as just as powerful, but also as deadly and as much a perversion of the great classic love stories as anything created by

Samuel Richardson. "Though life at its beginning was lovely as a corn of wheat, it was ground down to flour that must make bitter bread between two human tendencies: the insane sexual caprice of men, the not less mad excessive steadfastness of women."[13] Where in this world is there a place for the young, vibrant, loving Ellen? What possibility is there for a Suffragette to change what are viewed here as basic antagonistic male and female characteristics? In its view of basic human relationships, *The Judge* is the most pessimistic of Rebecca West's novels.

To what extent Rebecca West may be expressing in this novel the frustrations of her private life can only be surmised. She does create a long list of parallels between her own life and those of her characters. Ellen Melville's mother is Scottish, her father Irish. The father dies early, leaving the mother and daughter in poverty. Ellen is the youngest child in the family. She did well in school and later attended a Ladies College. She reads good books, is familiar with art and music, responds to natural beauty. She is alert to political issues and is a Suffragette. All of this reads persuasively like the life and character of the young Cicily Fairfield. Ellen's best girl friend, Rachel Wing (the familiar initials R.W.), even goes to London to study acting, and the man Ellen loves is older and extensively experienced with women.

Marion presents fewer parallels, but they are important. She too loves an older, experienced man and has an illegitimate son by him. Whatever other parallels can be drawn from Marion's situation can be only speculations as to what could have passed through the imagination of Rebecca West as she found herself in an exposed social situation, unmarried with a small child, and often alone. The too intense, almost unnatural bond between Marion and her son, Richard, is intriguing, suggestive of an effort to compensate here for what was felt to be Marion's rejection by her lover, or a defense of her commitment to an unorthodox relation by her attachment to the pledge of that relationship. One is tempted to read *The Judge* as an act of exorcism. Even so, one must recognize that it is an ambitious work; just as an example of technique it demonstrates how much West had advanced in the craft of fiction.

III   Harriet Hume

Rebecca West waited seven years before she published her next novel, *Harriet Hume* (1929), bracketing it by two books which she uses to summarize, at this stage, her critical thought, *The Strange Necessity* (1928) and *Ending in Earnest* (1931). In style this novel is a new departure, what she called "A London Fantasy." Fantasy for her seems to be stimulated in part by a dislocation in time, an unwillingness to accept the contemporary world as it is, a marked break from the assumptions of her first two novels. It is of interest that, so conceived, *Harriet Hume* would have appeared the same year as Virginia Woolf's *Orlando,* which utilizes a dislocation in both time and sex. Peter Wolfe does not think highly of *Harriet Hume;* in his view it falls short of the critical requirements Rebecca West set for fantasy. Similarly, Frank Swinnerton criticized Virginia Woolf's *Orlando,* describing it as a "calculatedly original work (but calculated originality is for me a contradiction in terms)."[14] The dissatisfaction of both critics seems to lie in what they view as an ineptness in trying to present things as they are not. In her study of Henry James, Rebecca West criticized him for wandering in a temporal Pays de Cockaigne, displaying continually, she thought, his lack of an historical sense. But he too delighted in the kind of fantasy that blurred the realization pressing continually in on us that we cannot escape that moment in which we exist. In her first novel Rebecca West has her soldier suffer from amnesia, a temporal escape that doctors can diagnose and cure. In his "fantasies" Henry James did not feel a requirement to stick to medical facts, yet his stories are still satisfying in their psychological verity. West's *Harriet Hume* is less so.

If fantasy is thought of as technique, the verbal play of the imagination, then we approach closer to the problem we face while reading this novel. One is confronted, page after page, with the play of Rebecca West's fancy unanchored by that attention to the here-and-now that gives balance and stability to her best work. H. G. Wells enjoyed the book. He wrote to West: "You've got your distinctive fantasy and humour into it, and it gives play for just the peculiar intricate wittiness which is one of your most delightful and inimitable characteristics."[15] But he knew intimately the mind and milieu out of which this fantasy was spun. His synapses functioned where ours may not. To take one obvious example, this is a *London* fantasy, so one must be able to recognize the allusions to that city and respond with not just "Ah, yes, I know," but with "Ah, yes, I understand." But whether the topic is London or something else, the expectation extends beyond knowledge to suggestive association, and the reader is expected to follow the significance of fancy's light-footed leaps here, there, and wherever.

Harriet Hume is based on the relationship between Harriet Hume and Arnold Condorex. Harriet is suggestive of that butterfly frivolity Ellen Melville characterized as an English quality. She is trim of ankle, small of hand, a "white witch," a spinner of symbolic tales, fey, a musician, and also the arbiter of morality in this novel. She has the terrifying gift of being able to know the thoughts of a person she loves. This means that Arnold Condorex can hide nothing from her, which makes this fantasy sometimes take on the character of a homily. Arnold Condorex is a man determined to succeed in politics, using whatever means he must. He appears at first as her lover, but abandons that role for an advantageous marriage. He blinds himself to morality, choosing instead advancement and advantage, consoling himself that he is not so bad as one of his colleagues. He builds his career on fabrication, his imagined city of Mondh, but loses the affection and trust of his colleagues in the process. The relationship of this woman and man consists of a series of meetings set at long intervals from each other. The novel begins with the two characters in the close relationship of lovers, then describes their increasing alienation, ending with their final reconciliation. The novel begins with Arnold seeking Harriet, gradually shifts to Harriet seeking Arnold, and then concludes with Arnold returning (as a spirit?) to Harriet.

Sister Mary Margarita Orlich identifies the theme of the novel as "the limited perfection that is imposed by the human condition."[16] Neither Harriet nor Arnold is perfect. but that imperfection is, as in *The Judge*, more characteristic of the man than of the woman. The setting supports this distinction, for an early scene in the novel is set in an Eden-like garden, but the garden is an annex of Harriet's house, and Arnold is the one who transgresses and must leave, not Harriet. His transgression, though, is not motivated by sexual caprice, as it was in *The Judge*, but by the pressure of social convention as that convention had been used by those older feminists, George Sand and Madame de Staël. Arnold sacrifices love for success and then realizes that the taste it leaves is bitter indeed. Harriet's imperfections do not originate in malice or effect injury to others, Arnold's imperfections do.

If woman versus man is a primary device West uses for

developing *Harriet Hume*, another significant device is the artist versus the politician, the creator versus the doer. The alienation between these two basic activities and the kinds of people who effect them Henry James had used as the theme of his novel *The Tragic Muse* which West read in preparation for her study of James. Her comments on the novel express a lack of sympathy that denigrates the significance of this conflict as James described it. He opts for the artist, as does Rebecca West, but he does not develop as strong a contrast or portray the decadent morality of politics so scathingly as she does. Perhaps tje difference lies in the characters employed. James centers his conflict in a male character who has the potential to be both politician and artist, but must choose between them. West splits the two vocations between a man and a woman. The effect is to make vocational distinctions on what are not necessarily relevant sexual differences.

Still, fruits of her thinking on art which had ripened over the years can be found here. Why Rebecca West should have accepted the assumption that the artist is so peripheral, so alien a part of modern civilization is a question that should be asked. If Henry James can be seen as an early version of the alienated artist and T. S. Eliot as continuing his tradition in West's generation, then H. G. Wells can be viewed as an example of the artist as the activator of social and political opinion, and Rebecca West continues that same intent in much of what she did. But Harriet seems to ally herself with the tradition of James, not Wells. As artist, Harriet can act as conscience, but her effect is minimal and temporary. She cannot legislate, though she can distinguish truth and can provide a refuge, and does both. West seems to have developed here a social perception of art that has problematic relations to her repudiation of Eliot and her reservations about James.

Art does have positive qualities in *Harriet Hume*. It is beauty that endures, whether as a sonata by Mozart or a house built by the Adams brothers. Harriet has the capacity to appreciate all art; Arnold can accept it as architecture but dislikes it as music. Whether West is employing a scale here with *applied* at one end and *pure* at the other is not clear; the Adams house in which Arnold lives is an appropriate setting for his political eminence, but he loves it with an absorption that seems to have nothing to do with politics. Art also is order, a means of ameliorating the chaos, of holding the uncertainties and accidents of life at bay. It is inward-looking, quick to catch out the fake, the specious, and unresponsive to the faddish, the popular. It is infused with meaning that is apparent to the discerning, but therein lies the hazard of intellectualization. In art, meaning without feeling is an arid dead-end. Harriet attracts first and last because she can love and be loved in return, and to try to separate her as woman from her as artist is to destroy both. Arnold, who had sought fame and greatness, sets out on his perilous journey back to her with the intent to destroy her, but instead secures a joyful refuge full of music and laughter, set in the effulgence of a returning spring.

But to say this is to end on a more comfortable stance with *Harriet Hume* than seems appropriate. Fantasy is not the mode in which Rebecca West is most effective. The fantasy has a strong element of satire in it, satire which would have been more successful if it had not been also arch and fey. Critics have often commented on the masculine qualities of West's work, by which, in part, they seem to be relying on the convention that man is characterized by reason and woman by feeling. In commenting on the novelist Clemence Dane, West makes also a distinction between male and female, but relies for the difference on the male novelist's ability to be natural, himself, and the female novelist's compulsion to be self-conscious, a contrivance.[17] Wells thought the fantastic mode West used in this novel was distinctively hers, but it should be remembered that in feminist matters Rebecca West did not think Wells was to be trusted. He could very well have admired just that contrived quality that West condemned in Clemence Dane's work. In other of her works West does lapse into passages comparable to the style of *Harriet Hume*, but these passages jar a presentation that elsewhere is different in tone and concept. If we use the measure West sets up for Clemence Dane, it is difficult to be certain how much of *Harriet Hume* is the work of a novelist and how much is the work of a female novelist.

Rebecca West's early novels show her willing to experiment with a variety of fictive materials and yet not be distinctively different in her methods from most other writers of the period. She does not give one the impression that she was seeking a formula that one could look at and identify as hers, nor does her literary personality appear strong enough to put its distinctive mark on everything she does, as is characteristic of the work of

Lawrence or Joyce or Woolf. These novels are too different, each from the other, to permit that. She does, however, display certain predilections in her choice of situation and characters. She prefers to present her fiction from the perspective of the feminine consciousness and uses elements of the sentimental novel when it suits her, but the fatalistic attitude toward the heroine present in that conventional novel is broadened by West to be a statement about all sexuality itself. Man is fickle, woman is faithful, and there is not much either of them can do to change their natures.

What continuity there is between these early novels and her later work comes from *The Return of the Soldier* and *The Judge* rather than from *Harriet Hume.* Her third novel is too light, too unfraught with consequence to reflect her usual state of mind, so it remains a sport that she tried once and then let rest without issue. The two earlier novels more closely resemble the topics and attitudes she will present later in *The Thinking Reed* and *The Fountain Overflows.*

CHAPTER 6

Novelist: Later Achievements

I   War Nurse

IN 1930 a book was published titled *War Nurse*. It purports to be "The True Story of a Woman Who Lived, Loved and Suffered on the Western Front."[1] This book appeared first in serial form in *Cosmopolitan* magazine, where the authorship was attributed to Rebecca West as told to her by the woman who had lived these experiences. It was a true story; West's contribution was only to put in more readable form what had been told to her. Having done this, she was not satisfied with it. She understood it would not be published. However, *Cosmopolitan* did publish it, attaching her name to it. She protested, and did succeed in keeping her name off from the book and movie that were produced later. Though this story is not of Rebecca West's creation, it does have some elements—American characters, wealth, international settings—which she was using in the short stories she was writing in this same period.

II   The Harsh Voice

These stories she wrote for magazine publication and then collected in *The Harsh Voice* (1935). *The Harsh Voice consists of* four short novels, three of which she had published earlier in *Saturday Evening Post* and *Woman's Home Companion*. Their appearance in these American magazines is indicative of a more general trend in her professional life. For a decade Rebecca West had been publishing her work with increasing frequency in the United States, a practice that developed naturally out of her growing personal familiarity with America and her acceptance by American readers. That she would have chosen, though, to

portray in these stories written in the early 1930s only those
Americans intent on seeking money raises the criticism that she
was not reacting responsively, as other writers had done, to an
America deep in a depression and suffering, as a consequence, a
paroxysm of social consciousness. In 1935 her stories still show
more affinity with the early F. Scott Fitzgerald than they do with
someone more representative of the 1930s like John Steinbeck.

In its portrayal of personal relations between a woman and a
man, *The Harsh Voice* does have its roots in the author's previous
fiction. She views that relationship not so much as a battle as a
contest characterized by a series of misunderstandings and
misconceptions. In part the problem lies where West placed it in
The Judge, with the irreconcilable differences between man and
woman. In these stories, though, it is more general: an ability to
rationalize evil into good, a realization that opposites both
attract and repel, an awareness that misunderstanding is the
norm of human relations. One story, "The Salt of the Earth," the
only non-American story in the collection, portrays a woman's
inability to understand the motives and consequences of her "do
good" actions. In another story, "The Abiding Vision," a man
caught up in the American dream of success cannot accept the
fact that that dream does not correspond with his own physical
mortality. In the two remaining stories, "Life Sentence" and
"There Is No Conversation," the woman is better at business
than her male counterpart, though not necessarily happier. Both
women have that foresight, shrewdness, and ruthlessness that
succeed on Wall Street, N.Y.C., or Main Street, U.S.A. These
women, Josephine Dickson Lambert and Nancy Sarle, live out
the American dream of material success; they make fortunes in
real estate, they manipulate the stock market, they outclass the
men at what the men thought was their own game. Their roles
are masculine; in balance, the roles of their men are characteristically feminine. The fact that women dominate their
financial worlds in these two stories creates an impression of a
society moving toward androgynous characteristics, its sexual
distinctions in flux. In *The Mauve Decade* Thomas Beer
portrayed the domineering woman of the end of the nineteenth
century as a willful, indomitable dowager and Philip Wylie
coined the term "Momism" to portray a later, equally dominant
female. Perhaps because Rebecca West is seeing the managerial
American woman through British feminist eyes she chooses to

change the overbearing woman portrayed by Beer and Wylie into someone more accepting of parity among equals and can place her in activities that contribute to that parity.

III   The Thinking Reed

Rebecca West's next novel, *The Thinking Reed,* published in 1936, completes the phase of her fiction begun by *The Harsh Voice.* It continues the international theme, though the interest shifts sharply from American to French culture. It continues as well West's skeptical analysis of the very wealthy, their characteristics and their significance. She described her purpose in writing this novel about rich people as a desire "to find out why they seemed to me as dangerous as wild boars and pythons."[2] Henry James wrote novels about the same class of people, but he assumed that wealth was a prerequisite for personal freedom. West would not argue with James's perception of the personal liberty created by wealth, but she would argue with his terms. James's "freedom" becomes "self-indulgence" to West; what for James is an asset becomes a hazard to her. She is closer to F. Scott Fitzgerald in her sense of what money does to people, except that again a qualification is necessary. Wild boars and pythons do not suffer from the soft rot of decadence; their impulse is to savage and destroy.

This view of the novel, though, must be balanced against the passage from Pascal's *Penseés* from which West derived her title *The Thinking Reed.* She quotes the passage as an epigraph:

Man is but a reed, the most feeble thing in nature; but he is a thinking reed. The entire universe need not arm itself to crush him. A vapour, a drop of water, suffices to kill him.But if the universe were to crush him, man would still be more noble than that which killed him, because he knows that he dies and the advantage which the universe has over him; the universe knows nothing of this.[3]

The image of man presented by Pascal ennobles him beyond the animalistic analogue West used to characterize her novel, but it is this often unequal battle between man as thinker and man as beast that is one of West's interests in this novel.

The plot of the novel is not complicated. Isabelle Terry, a young, wealthy American, recently widowed, comes to France to try to find distraction from her grief. She is attracted to a French aristocrat, André de Verviers, but soon discovers that he takes perverse pleasure in disordering her expectations. She seeks to replace him with the calm placidity of a Virginian, Lawrence Vernon, but, losing this refuge, turns to a dynamic exponent of modern French industrialism, Marc Sallafranque, and marries him. She conceives a child, but loses it by miscarriage. Falling into a depression, she seeks a divorce, but, realizing her commitment is to her husband, she returns to him. This plot has the kind of simplicity that lends itself to psychological analysis of character. West uses it for that, but also finds it convenient for two other purposes: to analyze what it means to be rich, and to describe what it means to be a woman.

In this novel the international theme is used to provide Isabelle with the opportunity to discover a new world, France, but this process of discovery is not effected simply by contrasting America with France, as West had done earlier in her story "There Is No Conversation." Isabelle's ancestry is French; her family had clung to its cultural distinctiveness even though it had dwelt in St. Louis, Missouri, for generations. So Isabelle's predisposition is to slough off what makes her different. Her only significant tie to her American past is her guardian-counselor Uncle Honoré, who intrudes only in the form of letters filled with business documents and advice which we neither read nor hear repeated. So Isabelle is remarkably free, free to create her own happiness or misfortune, whichever she has the genius to accomplish.

In his study of Rebecca West, Peter Wolfe has pointed out the similarities between Henry James's heroines like Milly Theale and Isabel Archer and Rebecca West's Isabelle Terry Sallafranque. The differences are just as important. Whereas James's heroines find their European world primarily among American expatriates and Britains, Rebecca West's Isabelle assimilated into a French world which, in those places where the wealthy congregate, meant an amalgam of nationalities. What happens to Isabelle has little to do with her being American or with her being an innocent in the Jamesian sense. It does have to do essentially with her learning more about herself as an individual and a woman, and how to use that knowledge to manage whatever situation she may find herself in. It has to do also with her final realization that her happiness is dependent on her ability to diminish her capacity for self-delusion and selfish desire. The marriages of Isabel Archer and Isabelle Sallafranque were similar in that they both married for self-deluded reasons, each unaware of the nature of the man she married. Both of them conceived a child and lost it. Both were tempted to escape their marriages and both, acting out of moral exigency, returned.

So there are similarities, but one remaining difference almost nullifies them by itself. Henry James portrayed a lady; Rebecca West presents a woman. The distinction between James's lady and West's woman is most evident in what each author does with that uniquely feminine experience, the conceiving and bearing of a child. James moves hurriedly over Isabel's marriage, the birth of her child, and its death, collapsing these momentous events into a few pages in the middle of the novel, almost losing them between huge narrative blocks portraying Isabel's mental progress toward her destiny. Rebecca West builds her novel toward that period in which Isabelle is pregnant with child. The climax of the novel comprises her loss of that child and the consequences of that loss on her marriage. James's lady can, in another of his novels, be a gentleman; his interest in Isabel is not in her uniquely feminine experiences. Rebecca West's interest in Isabelle does center in those experiences that are hers because she is a woman. James's reticence about childbearing is almost complete. Rebecca West also preserves some reticence, particularly about its physiological aspects, but we do witness their effects, the sense Isabelle has of the miracle working inside her and the empty depression she suffers when she loses it. In her effort to make the feminine experience acceptable as art West has moved significantly beyond James.

To return to the interest West has in common with James, a search for moral stability, Isabelle believes that her husband and the French civilization he exemplifies can help her to those moral riches she seeks. She who had been so much alone learns that French civilization emphasizes the close interplay of human relations characteristic of a small community. Even though she was living in Paris, she gradually realized that this great city was "also a village, where countless metropolitans follow unaltered village ways"[4] which permitted them to be "all splendidly themselves."[5] These Parisians enjoyed each other, their life together, and took the proper occasions to show it. They valued "the good meat of common sense"[6] mutually shared, which means, among other things, thrift and moderation and a sense of personal and communal responsibility. Here one could not deal in selfish excesses. "There was nothing casual about life in France, it demanded perpetually that one should hit the note in the middle."[7]

What takes her longest to recognize is the respectful understanding the French have for a woman as woman. She becomes aware of this attitude first in their art. She attends a play which

was simply written to exhibit an actress who was neither beautiful nor very young, but who had the gift of remembering exactly what it has been like to pass through the characteristic stages of a woman's life in a society dominated by Christian ideas of sex, to be a virgin and to be taken by a man, to be pursued and to be abandoned, to be deceived and to deceive, to be happy and to outlive the concept of happiness.[8]

In this drama actress and spectators united in interest; over them "arched a consolidating national ideal"[9] that would have been impossible in an American or British play about a woman because there a variety of social vectors would have infected the simple purity of interest the French play had. As it was in the play, so Isabelle finally realized it was in her marriage.

If French civilization is a source of order and the good life, other elements stimulate disorder. Of these disruptive elements, the most important is wealth. Rich people, particularly idle rich people, are presented as determined to obliterate all standards, all order, all purposeful effort except that which contributes to their self-satisfaction. Their wealth has insulated them from the discipline that our limited resources force on most of us. The glut of possibilities they enjoyed induced in them the impulse "to treat life so that it would never form any pattern, to rub down each phenomenon till it became undistinguishable from all others of its kind."[10] This desperate need for diversion is responsible in part for the characterization, "wild boars and pythons," West gave them. They slash and they crush because they must get through days that can give them no more than what a hundred days before had provided, and they end those days in the desperate excitement of the gambling casinos. In part, though, they are wild boars and pythons because they retain vestigial impulses from their fathers and grandfathers,

who succeeded in seizing that wealth because they were cunning
and ruthless.

What a nullity of mind and spirit these rich parasites present.
Though they are living through the political upheavals of the
1920s, neither they nor any of the others who move with them in
coveys from one watering place to another, from one enervating
diversion to another, show any potential for resistance to the
threat building in Central Europe. Germans and Italians hardly
exist in this novel; as nations they represent only vague irritants.
Perhaps they did not serve West's purpose, but their absence
seems foreboding. Marc Sallafranque's automobile factory exists
because the government let it be built only on the proviso that it
be quickly convertible to the manufacture of war materials.
There are also dark suspicions of foreign subversives creating
labor disturbances in France. But Marc Sallafranque sees these
intrusions into his affairs as nothing more than annoying
hindrances; his ambition is to reduplicate his cheap, efficient,
little automobile as many times as he can. He sees this as
adequate service to his community. Isabelle's response is not
significantly greater. *The Thinking Reed* ends with her awareness of the impending stock market crash in the United States,
but she hardly reacts. She has seen enough of this purgatorial
world of rich parasites to contemplate the possibility of change
as not worse than what exists, but paradoxically looks forward as
well to conceiving and mothering children who will have their
existence in a world she can foresee only dimly.

IV   The Fountain Overflows

For twenty years Rebecca West did not publish another novel.
The war she had feared came and went. She began her study of
traitors and published what she found. Honors began to come to
her. She was made a member of the American Academy of Arts
& Sciences and received an honorary degree from New York
University. She was made a Chevalier of the Legion of Honour in
1957; in 1959 she was made a Dame of the British Empire.
Between these last two honors, in 1958, she published *The
Fountain Overflows*, serializing it first in *Ladies' Home Journal*
and then publishing it as a book. It is a large novel of memories, a
novel about childhood, with its uneasy fears and aspirations. It
reads as if the author had reached that stage in her life when she

wanted to look back, not so much to reminisce about the past as to come to terms with it. The topics found in this novel often appear to be activated by deep-seated, emotional commitments rooted in her feminine sensibility and her difficult childhood.

The novel was a popular success, as it should have been, because it is full of incident and characters, and has a sensational murder woven into it. The story is told from the point of view of Rose, a child. It opens in Scotland, where Clare Aubrey, the mother, is to stay with her four children, Cordelia, Rose, Mary, and Richard Quin, while her husband, Piers Aubrey, travels to London to prepare for an editor's job. This is the last of a series of jobs he has had and lost in Britain and far countries of the world, in part because he is unreliable, in part because he irritates people with his attitude of superiority. When she fails to hear from her husband, Clare must take the children alone to London. There life begins well enough. The father wins some fame and fortune as a pamphleteer and a promoter of causes, but later his speculating in stocks reduces his family to poverty. The mother, a former concert pianist, teaches music to her children, particularly to two of her daughters, Rose and Mary, whom she thinks have musical ability. She encourages Richard Quin as well, but only tolerates Cordelia's efforts to learn the violin because she is certain Cordelia has no musical talent. A cousin named Jock, his wife, Constance, and daughter Rosamund are brought into the story to serve as analogous supports for the Aubrey family. The mother of a schoolmate of the children murders her husband. Piers Aubrey involves himself in the trial proceedings in an attempt to effect what he considers to be a larger social benefit. He succeeds. But his family life continues to disintegrate; he becomes increasingly estranged until one day he deserts his family. By selling some family portraits the mother succeeds in keeping the family together until Rose and Mary are capable of beginning their careers as concert pianists. Richard Quin will do well because he is both accomplished and socially adept. Only Cordelia is troubled. She learns that she lacks the ability to become a competent violinist and must adjust to more commonplace expectations. This summary suggests something of the story's complexity, but it does no justice to the excitement and interest the novel generates in the reader's mind.

In its use of themes basic to West's thinking *The Fountain Overflows* resembles *The Judge* more than any other of her novels, though there are thirty-four years between their publication dates. The fundamental difference between men and women that is stated in the conclusion of *The Judge*—men are capricious, women are steadfast—is as significant a theme in *The Fountain Overflows* as it is in *The Judge,* but with one qualification; the difference is not expressed in sexual activity. Rose's father has strong convictions and great gifts of persuasion, but he feels compelled to use them in efforts that foster his desire for martyrdom, with no thought for the consequences to his family. He is equally incapable of managing a stable economic existence. Uncertain even as to where his emotional commitments lie, he can extend great kindnesses to comparative strangers when at the same time he closes himself away from his own family. Cousin Jock also exemplifies instability. He has a good salary, but he too denies his family adequate financial support. Because he feels this life is so horrible, he makes a parody of it with his vulgar conduct, and he dabbles in spiritualism. If the fathers represent only instability, that perhaps could be managed, but they can be tyrannous as well. To the children they present models of unapproachable achievement, but also threatening potentials of insecurity and disruption at a time when those children are most vulnerable. In retrospect Rose concludes, "I had a glorious father, I had no father at all."[11]

The mothers Clare and Constance stand as guardian angels, protecting their children from the chaos and vulgarity of the world, calming when they can, exhorting when they must, supporting the potential for unique distinction in each of their children. They love, cherish, and obey their husbands, but when they must choose absolutely between husband and child, a choice for them between fostering death or life, they prefer the child and aspirant life. Constance is calm, monumental. Clare is electric, driving. Both have a distinction that separates them from the ordinary, the commonplace. This distinction is not related to status or wealth; it is an inner gift, a belief in oneself, an ability to recognize excellence and a determination to promote it where possible.

In its portrayal of the skimping, make-do life of the poor, *The Fountain Overflows* has qualities like those one finds in the fiction of Arnold Bennett or George Moore, but basically this is not a novel about the poor, it is a novel about genius, about its recognition, its cultivation, its achievement. Clare Aubrey is a gifted musician, a concert pianist who gave up her career for marriage. She recognizes the same musical gifts in her two daughters, Mary and Rose. By her example and patient guidance she brings them to the point where they can determine their own professional destinies. This patient cultivation of the potential for distinctive excellence has its own process and standards. There is a terrifying finality about the initial distinction; the fortunate few are gifted, the rest are not. The religious exclusiveness of the elect does not winnow with any greater absoluteness than does the artistic selectivity of the gifted. There is no mistake and there is no recourse. But if one is of the select company, one has a capacity for self-sustenance that makes the harshness of existence peculiarly irrelevant.

"Be thankful for this oddity, which has brought you safe through terrible years. But do not think you owe it to any virtue in yourselves. You owe it entirely to your musical gifts. . . . If God had not made you able to play you would be as helpless as Cordelia, and it is not her fault but God's that she cannot play, and as God has no faults let us now drop the subject."[12]

What Clare Aubrey has said to her children here about music is equally true of any other gift. Art does create a way of life that matures and compensates its acolytes. Its rewards are not always visible, but of their kind they are abundant. Others would like to participate in those rewards, so art has its frauds and its hangers-on, but an artist can distinguish the true from the false with incorruptible infallibility. No musician sure of his own gift would accept Cordelia's violin-playing as authentic music and would not perjure himself to tell her that it was. *The Fountain Overflows* can be read as Rebecca West's celebration of the artist and his noble vocation.

The certainty that exists in this part of the novel is not so apparent elsewhere. On the dustcover of the Viking edition West stated that she thought the novel's theme "might be said to be the way that human beings look at each other inquisitively, trying to make out what is inside the opaque human frame." She does not assume that this theme is original with her. Instead, she continues: "St. Augustine says that human beings are disguised by their bodies, and that only God can look through 'the lattice of our flesh' to see what we are really like." She would have known

also Virginia Woolf's famous phrase "a semitransparent
envelope" by which Woolf identifies this same problem in human
perception. The impossibility of knowing the true nature of
anyone else intensifies the uncertainties the male element had
introduced already into the world of these children. Rose and
Mary may find security in their musical gift, but their relation
with their less gifted sister is clouded by painful, ambiguous
motives. Their bias blinds them to other genuine gifts she does
have. The uncertainties also lead to efforts, sometimes valid,
sometimes spurious, to turn that opaqueness into clarity. The
true self can be seen in moments of intense commitment, as Rose
realizes when she watches her father risk imprisonment to gain a
political achievement. But it cannot be seen by loving another, or
by long, intimate relation with another, or by the desperate
search for clairvoyance.[13] The more each is obsessed with
himself the less he sees of the nature of others. The great charm
of Richard Quin and Rosamund, who constantly are together in
this novel, is their ability to give of themselves, to reach out and
empathetically comprehend.

Not enough is known about Rebecca West's childhood to trace
the autobiographical sources of this novel with any precision.
The similarity of the family unit in *The Fountain Overflows* and
The Judge suggests that it is a creation with autobiographical
significance. An Anglo-Irish father, a Scots mother, three
daughters, and a son comprise the complete unit. All are present
in *The Fountain Overflows*. Of this unit only the mother and one
daughter have survived in *The Judge;* the others are only
memories. Except for the son, Rebecca West's family was the
same. She had two older sisters; one of them, Letitia Fairfield, to
whom *The Fountain Overflows* is dedicated, was a doctor of
medicine, paralleled here by Rosamund's desire to be a nurse.
The boy Richard Quin is named after his father's beloved
brother who died young. Rebecca West based her portrayal of
him on her mother's brother Joseph, a handsome, promising
musician who died in his early twenties. The games of fantasy the
children play have their duplicates in West's childhood. Her
negative response to formal schooling is duplicated in the
attitude of Rose. The attributes of distinction and eccentricity, of
being different from the commonplace, of having other than
commonplace interests, have also the suggestion of autobiography in them. The incident of the family portraits that are sold to

sustain the family after the father disappears duplicates West's memory of her father and mother looking at a portrait that hung above her bed when they were living in the London suburb of Streatham and her father saying, " 'I wonder if that is a genuine Lawrence. If it is it must be worth something.' " It was a genuine Lawrence and her mother sold it. West recalled that "we lived on the proceeds of that sale for a long time; and that speaks of some further achievement on the part of my mother, for it is miraculous that it should have been preserved from the stock-gambling mania of my father."[14]

The character of Piers Aubrey corresponds to that of West's father in point after point. Her father's mania for gambling haunted West. When years later she saw the jagged outline of desert mountains, she felt distress and insecurity. A psychologist later told her that she was associating the outline of the mountains with the graphs of the rise and fall of the copper market her father had left lying about. When she was a young woman she had seen her father as an aristocrat without the inner resources to use his background and education effectively. "More and more did his proceedings fail to crystalize into achievements, more and more did his personal life become a discontinuous string of episodes that were hardly events."[15] This was her view of her father when she was thirty-three years old, shortly after she had broken her relation with H. G. Wells. Rebecca West wrote another portrait of her father shortly after her seventieth birthday, six years after she had published *The Fountain Overflows*. In this portrait her bitterness has disappeared. In the earlier article she had dismissed him with the comment: "When the house is in ruins, when the ship is wrecked, there is nobody more helpless, more ignorant of any principle that might enable him to rebuild the house or refloat the ship, than the aristocrat."[16] In her later essay she tells of how her father was forced by his social position into the army, a profession for which he was not suited because he was, as his daughter described him, "George Bernard Shaw cubed."[17] His mind was a scintillation of ideas about many subjects, but mostly about politics and economics, and he enjoyed putting his theories into print. As a child his daughter absorbed those interests. She describes how he gave her the concept that the stability of this world existed only in the landscape and among animals. He taught her also that the world of human events changed for better or worse as the ideas that activated them changed. Perhaps the most difficult lesson she learned from her father was the need for stoicism. Perhaps the most enduring lessons she learned were to be excited about ideas and to desire to know.

During his lifetime my father was a little remote from me, because he was more intent on understanding than being understood; which is a good fault, but still a fault, in a parent. But in later years I come nearer to him every time I am concerned with people who ask searching questions and wait for the answers. . . .[18]

The fading of Rebecca West's earlier bitterness toward her father that one finds here is apparent already in the more tender quality with which she presents Piers Aubrey in *The Fountain Overflows*. She recognized both his superiority and his desire to use that superiority to good purposes. That he failed is a tragedy, not a sin.

Rebecca West thought both her parents were superior to her. She could admit her father's superiority only later in her life; from the beginning she did not question her mother's greatness. In her fiction mothers are always sources of strength. But also, women are superior to men, the Scots to the Irish, the musician to the politician and the pamphleteer. All her life Rebecca West wanted her mother's approval for what she did, and when she did not have it she suffered and tried to obscure her failure. Her mother was a source of moral strength. She was much more. "She had as much genius as any human I have ever encountered. . . . She was a miracle. She refused to be confounded by her hideous ill luck."[20] In *The Fountain Overflows* Clare Aubrey is a concert pianist who gave up her career for her marriage. Rebecca West's mother also was a professional pianist. West remembered her mother's sacrifice in sending her to concerts at which the pianists played no better than what she heard at home. Making Clare Aubrey a professional pianist can be read as West's desire to assert again what was her mother's earned privilege. It can be interpreted, as well, as her effort to put her mother in proper social and familial balance with the looming authority of her father. That of all the arts music was chosen to be celebrated in this novel again confirms the influence of the mother. One of Mrs. Fairfield's daughters turned to poetry, another to journalism and fiction. None of them made a serious commitment to music.

Clare Aubrey was more fortunate. Music is the focus of her children's lives, exemplifying an enhancement by the author of a treasured memory, a smoothing out of the awkward incongruities of reality to make them a fictive harmony.

The title of *The Fountain Overflows* is taken from the proverb "The cistern contains: the fountain overflows" in Blake's *The Marriage of Heaven and Hell*. The image of the fountain suggests energy, movement, abundance, generosity. This image recurs in the novel, but there it is associated with rage and pain.[20] Rage and pain, though, are only one aspect of this novel; they are not central, and they are mostly internalized. The fountain of memory overflows more profusely. This is a story of remembrance, of Rose's memory of what she experienced as a child. But as she concludes her story, the memory finds its expression in another image that seems to overwhelm her. "It was my father and mother who existed. I could see them as two springs, bursting from a stony cliff, and rushing down a mountainside in torrent, and joining to flow through the world as a great river. . . . I was swept on by the strong flood of which I was a part."[21] Though West demurred when asked about the autobiographical quality of her novel, one senses while reading it that she too was swept on by the strong flood of her parents.

V The Birds Fall Down

Two years after West published her final version of her study of traitors, *The New Meaning of Treason*, she published in 1966 her latest novel, *The Birds Fall Down*. It is a story that has its inception in the remarkable career of Azeff, a traitor who practiced his peculiar kind of treachery in the first decade of this century. He was an employee of the Russian secret police while simultaneously he was the head of the most powerful terrorist organization in Russia, playing off each group against the other for his own purposes. Unlike a double agent, he had no basic commitment to either group. West had known his story from her early years in London when she had heard it from Ford Madox Ford and his sister. She uses Azeff's treachery in *Black Lamb and Grey Falcon* as an example of the degeneration of the terrorist revolutionary movement in Russia before World War I. She compared his clever duplicity with the naive idealism of those Southern Slavic terrorists like Princip, the assassin of Franz

Ferdinand, who had convictions but lacked cunning and skill. Azeff's importance in history transcends his success as an assassin. Princips created history by killing; Azeff changed the course of history by being unmasked. The discovery of his treachery resulted in the disintegration of his group of revolutionaries and a shift of his power to Lenin. So what West recounts in her novel is a fictionalized version of a momentous event in modern history.

The theme West thought was important in *The Fountain Overflows*, our effort to see what is inside the opaque human frame of each other, is even more pervasive in *The Birds Fall Down*. What is seen as a human characteristic that the Aubrey family tries to mitigate becomes the professional *modus operandi* of many characters in *The Birds Fall Down*. The successful traitor is he who can conceal his identity as traitor from all except those few who must know. To succeed as a double traitor means deliberately to create two false identities with whatever hazards that may cause to the traitor's own perception of his identity. In the statement Klaus Fuchs wrote after his arrest he described the conscious, controlled state of schizophrenia in which he had to live and how it finally disintegrated when he began to feel affection for those around him. The double traitor would have to justify his actions by an act of personal rationalization unsupported by any social or political sanction. In *The New Meaning of Treason* West had discovered the possibility of the double traitor in the political limbo of West Berlin, but mostly she had examined only traitors who had exchanged one allegiance for another or who had adopted an allegiance early in life which later they concealed. The double traitor functions best in a country at war with itself. Thus an Azeff could prosper in a Russia on the eve of a revolution, and thus in her study of traitors West would not have found a British Azeff to serve as the source of her novel. The interest this complex act of treason could create seems to explain why for her fiction she preferred the double traitor to the traitor, the Russian anarchist to the British spy.

The story is told through the consciousness of an eighteen-year-old girl, Laura Rowan. Her mother, Tania, is the daughter of a Russian aristocrat, Count Nicolai Diakonov; her father, Edward Rowan, is a member of Parliament. Count Nicolai and his wife live in Paris in exile because the count, a former minister of justice, had failed to prevent Russian anarchists from assassinating several Russian officials. Monsieur Kamensky, an old colleague and friend, is his companion in his exile. The story centers on a trainride the count and his granddaughter take to visit a relative. On the train the count is approached by Chubinov, a revolutionary, who by comparing facts with the count determines that Kamensky is a double traitor who had betrayed the count and caused his exile. The shock to the count is so severe that he leaves the train and dies that evening in a hotel. Chubinov returns to Paris. Laura fears that Kamensky will kill her because of what she knows, so she sends Chubinov information that will enable him to assassinate Kamensky. Chubinov does kill him and Laura helps Chubinov conceal his crime.

The novel is rich in analogue and symbol. The primary plot has its treasonous parallel in the Rowan household, where Susie Staunton, Tania's friend, who hides her beauty and wealth behind an hypocrisy of self-effacement, consorts secretly with Tania's husband. The novel's title *The Birds Fall Down,* a reference to the hunting of birds, offers an opportunity for symbolic overlay that West uses, transferring the ceremonial quality of hunting scenes Count Nicolai remembers from Old Russia to the pursuit of the more dangerous game described in this novel. The atmosphere of Czarist Russia is richly recreated in the person of Count Nicolai. With his religious orthodoxy and absolute devotion to the czar, his delight in the discussion of doctrine, his intense states of feeling, his search for personal tests, his masculinity, he embodied many of the Slavic characteristics West had observed in her experience with the South Slavs. The care with which she recreates the world of the anarchists has a verisimilitude as great as Joseph Conrad achieved in *The Secret Agent* or Henry James in *The Princess Casamassima,* though she seems more willing to embed it in the density of history.

The characteristics of the traitor remain basically the same as they were in *The Meaning of Treason.* The traitor's worst crime is that he betrays those who trust him. The traitor who commits treason within the sanctuary of the home seems most perfidious, and both traitors in this novel are guilty of that crime. West's study of traitors would suggest to her that treason was primarily a male activity, a conclusion that she could support by her belief

in the instability of men and in her assumption that it was a male
characteristic to corrupt the seriousness of life by converting it
into a game, yet she gave Susie Staunton the same qualities.

West's study of traitors suggests also that treason is only a
political phenomenon. But earlier she had fought that assumption, and here much later she appears to deny it even more
emphatically than she had done before. She makes treason
intimate and personal to the point that the ultimate condemnation of traitors is that they cannot be loved. So they justify their
treason by other means. Kamensky plays a philosophical game by
finding a rationale for his actions in Hegel's dialectic process,
which satisfies his uneasiness but is so patently false that Laura's
instant response to it is, " 'Why, everybody knows that's
wrong.' "[22] Susie is no better, for she tries to justify her treachery
by her peevish sense that others have more than she does.
Kamensky cannot see what his own sins are, perhaps because his
greatest sin is pride. Count Nicolai, who is no traitor, can also
commit the sin of pride, but he is saved by his ability to curb his
egotism, countering it with a humility based in his religious
belief. Kamensky and Susie Staunton also appear to have
humility, but for them it is only a mask. To Kamensky this is only
one mask among many. He can be all men to all people. Mime is
his stock in trade, as it is for other traitors, but neither he nor
they seem to realize the total effect their imitation of reality has
on those they wish to deceive. For them consequences are
difficult to project beyond the temporary reflex of action and
response. For their victims consequences resolve themselves into
some more durable realization. The traitors' masks made them
variable; in themselves they are indistinct. "When Susie was
looking up like that, one could see how long her throat was, and
how curious her mouth, so indeterminate, so hard to describe or
remember."[23] Kamensky's undistinguished face makes him even
less distinct; he has an appearance so ordinary that "hundreds of
thousands look exactly as he does."[24] So he and she can practice
their deceptions with assurance that they can pass undetected. A
man looking like any other can behave like Satan and no cloven
hoof will betray him. Only time can erode his disguise.

That this traitorous perfidy must be witnessed through the
awakening awareness of an eighteen-year-old girl forces the
reader to judge it with a perception attuned to a more absolute
sense of right and wrong than would have been possible from

someone older, more world-weary, more cynical. Laura learns
for the first time how fear and grief actually feel. She learns that
treachery is not fought successfully by frankness. Even for her,
deception works better. If she is to win the battle, the price she
will pay is loss of innocence. She learns that security may be
lacking where she most expects it. Her own father may pass
before her eyes unknowingly into the camp of the enemy and her
mother may lack the perceptiveness necessary to save her. She
must finally violate her concept of herself if she is to survive. All
of this she learns in France, the most civilized of countries, where
that very civility is a hazard because the terror is loose in the
guise of civility. She must recognize the traitor even in a frock
coat or a modest black dress. She must recognize the ironic fact
that the Russian culture loved by her mother and grandfather, a
culture which created the icon her grandfather cherishes above
all things, also could so thoroughly embrace the art of disguise.
Where does truth lie, and can one recognize it if one sees it?

This is a cruel world for a young woman to live in. It is a vastly
different world from that of Ellen Melville or Marion Yaverland
in *The Judge*, where they do face the threat of a sexual menace
that may violate and disgrace them, but they do not face
annihilation because chance has thrust into their keeping
knowledge they do not necessarily want. The world of the traitor
is indifferent to everything a young woman may cherish. It is a
world in which youth is a hazard, not an asset; beauty is an
indifferent quality; and ardor is replaced by conviction that has
its source in the impulse toward death.

The reader does not leave *The Birds Fall Down* with anything
like the comforting assurance that he can find in *The Fountain
Overflows*. In that novel youth wins through to successful
achievement. At the end of *The Birds Fall Down* an innocent
maiden has witnessed the failure of her parents' marriage and
has been an accomplice to murder. Her eyes are turned east to
Russia, where she expects security and exoneration for her
mother's family name. Yet in Russia she will find a revolution
that may destroy her or, at best, force her into exile. The novel's
conclusion reverberates with the ironies of history.

The Birds Fall Down is an impressive conclusion to the series
of novels Rebecca West has written. She found in this novel a
format better suited to her special blend of telling and stating
than in any of her other novels. She created a story rich in

character and taut with suspense. Despite the resemblance of its
subject to that of a Graham Greene "entertainment," this it is
not; the solidity with which it is set in the actualities of time and
place, the informedness and wisdom of it, prevent its being
classified in that popular category. But we should not expect it to
be because West is not inclined to imitation, either of herself or
of others. Even at the age of seventy-four she demonstrated that
she was developing as an artist and was willing to try something
new. This in itself is an achievement not many authors can equal.

Aside from her determination to improve and to be original,
West presents evidence here of her effort to move gradually
away from personal experience. Her early novels are rooted
emotionally in her relation with H. G. Wells. But in *Harriet Hume*
she detached her fiction from that turbulent, personal experience, and in *The Thinking Reed* she created her fiction as much
from her interpretation of the contemporary economic and
political situation as she did from her awareness of herself as a
woman. In *The Fountain Overflows* she did return to private
experience, but it is a harkening back to the remote past of her
childhood. The pull of this memory must have been strong,
because her impulse carried her to the point of conceiving the
history of the Aubrey family as a trilogy. However, she published
only the first novel of this trilogy, which in its conclusion—the
children entering adulthood—releases the tension that would
seem to have motivated the whole ambitious project.[25] Of all her
novels, *The Birds Fall Down* is most clearly divorced from the
author's personal experiences. It demonstrates most evidently a
fictive reworking of an interest developed from observation and
reading. Looking at the whole sequence of novels West has
written, we find that the hortatory and expiational impulses
ebbed as the urge to know surged and encompassed more. The
final view she presents is not just of an individual life, but
encompasses an age.

Not all of Rebecca West's fiction will endure. The desire of
Evelyn Hutchinson and Sister Orlich, two critics who have
written favorably of her fiction, to find special merit in novels
like *The Judge* or *Harriet Hume* is based on justifications other
than artistic merit. If West had attempted an orderly development of fictive technique early in her career instead of moving
from the realism of *The Judge* to the fantasy of *Harriet Hume* to
the satire of *The Thinking Reed*, that development could have

reached a higher achievement more rapidly. But her interests were pulled in too many directions and her energies were diverted into too many diverse projects to make this possible. The kind of fiction she writes well is a careful construct made from an accumulation of research and thoughtful consideration. Her fictive genius owes more to meditation than it does to inspiration. The novel which best displays evidence of this kind of careful, prolonged nurture is *The Birds Fall Down*. Following closely behind it is *The Fountain Overflows*. These two novels come closer than any of West's other fiction to matching her achievement in *Black Lamb and Grey Falcon* and *The New Meaning of Treason*. They are substantial achievements and deserve to be remembered.

CHAPTER 7

Conclusion

W HEN Rebecca West was created Dame of the British
Empire in 1959 she had achieved a distinction that would
have been difficult to have foreseen when in 1912 she published
her first article in the *Freewoman*. To be recognized with this
kind of honor from a government which almost half a century
earlier she had abused violently and persistently in the public
press indicates that significant changes had occurred both for
her and for Britain. She was a rebel made, not a rebel born. Her
early life was not conducive to contentment. The poverty, the
illness from tuberculosis, the loss of her father: they all spelled
misfortune. But like Rose in *The Fountain Overflows* she was not
soft. As a young maiden she was already trying to make her way
in a world that was not sure it wanted to permit her to do so. She
rushed into life, desiring all of it and taking tremendous risks in
trying to obtain it. She made mistakes and suffered for them. For
many years British society would not forgive her for snatching
what happiness she could from her love for H. G. Wells. Yet she
persisted and finally won her way through to acceptance and a
measure of contentment.

Like the British women during World War I, she earned
Britain's admiration by her steadfast support of her country
during its second, more terrible ordeal, World War II. Earlier,
during the 1930s, her dedication was just as true, but Britain
thought hers was the voice of Cassandra largely lost in a droning
chorus of the complacent. Like her father, she spoke but was not
heeded. As Britain passed through the early agonies of World
War II, Rebecca West was experiencing her own agony of
writing *Black Lamb and Grey Falcon,* making it both a
celebration and a knell of doom. She described in it her distress
at seeing the world she knew disappear into the maw of
destruction the totalitarian dictators had opened. The war ended
with Britain victorious, but victory did not mean a return to life

as it had been. Again West sensed the change and again she found the sensitive spot to probe and examine. She studied the traitors; she created her gallery of portraits and set them against the backdrop of British institutions and British traditions. This was a salutary service to her country. If for nothing more than her contribution to British political well-being, she properly belonged on the 1959 Honors List as Dame of the British Empire.

Dame Rebecca's most useful contribution to literary criticism has been her long years of service as an arbiter of publishers' wares. She read everything and she expressed supportable opinions of what she read. Much of her work as a reviewer of books was little more than labor, but she read thoughtfully and she remembered what she read. When we reexamine that series of longer, reflective essays she wrote for the *Herald Tribune* and the memorials she composed for Henry James, Arnold Bennett, and D. H. Lawrence, we can appreciate both her critical acumen and her craft. For her, literary artists are members of a community which has its own unique standards and rules. Those who would be authors must respect the word, its beauty and its integrity. If possible they should be wise, but at least they should display some grace of mind and charm of spirit. Literary artists are also members of a larger community and owe responsiblities to it. To state, as Dame Rebecca does in the conclusion to *The Court and the Castle,* that literature above a certain level generally speaks to the communal concerns of statecraft and religion would require that the artists who create that literature be in and of that community, not perhaps as legislators as the poet Shelley desired, but at least as observers and preferably as participants. Her criticism expresses her concern that artists should not assume that they can isolate their aesthetic interests from other intellectual interests of this larger community. What Henry James and James Joyce had to offer was important, and it was of value to study them until one had come to terms with them and understood their relation to the literary tradition. But what Sigmund Freud and Ivan Pavlov had to contribute was equally important. If artists and literary critics ignored them, they did so at their own risk. In West's view, literature is not separable from life; it is one of life's finest manifestations. Good criticism concerns itself with both. In doing so, the process criticism follows is, first, to try to establish order from the confusion it encounters; second, to seek to illuminate; always it should champion the transcendent value of art.

Dame Rebecca values history almost as highly as she does art. Like art, history is an ordering of life which gives pleasure, but in its capacity to provide knowledge it is equally valuable. Rebecca West has a unique sensibility for how the past actually becomes present, how it has shaped the world we think is ours. Living in London stimulated so strongly in her the sense that past and present intermingle that she wrote her "London Fantasy" *Harriet Hume* in response to it. Everywhere she went in Yugoslavia she sensed that rather than the past merely being of use to the present—a cathedral to enter, a street to follow, a bridge to cross—the past was itself knowable. At the site of the Battle of Kossovo she relived the experience of Prince Lazar and the gray falcon and realized its consequences which were as vivid to her as was that other experience at the Sheep's Field where she felt a rush of the human spirit out of the past as it repeated the same sacrificial act over and over again in its urge to insure its temporal continuance. History does not spare us much of the agony of this life, but it can help us understand why that agony persists. We are not left in quite the darkness experienced by the old woman in the Montenegrin mountains who felt impelled to wander and question the meaning of her existence which, to Dame Rebecca, was encapsulated within the history of the Southern Slavs. It was a turbulent life within a turbulent history. Charles Fairfield taught his daughter not to fear change but, rather, to expect it, so Yugoslavian history seemed to her to epitomize better than most the nature of man's collective experience.

Dame Rebecca's concept of man's nature swings between two heresies, Pelagianism and Manicheanism, that serve as magnets to which her observations seem to be pulled. Her friend and critic Evelyn Hutchinson has stressed the more general anti-nomial characteristic of her work into which these two heresies fit. The brightness of the Pelagian perfect free will delighted her, but all her experience told her that it was a dangerous illusion. More often she was drawn by the evidence of circumstance and observation to the dark uncertainties of Manicheanism. The age in which she lived and her own experience did much to enhance its seeming validity. But her delight in life and her pleasure in the play of her own mind kept her from embracing it. Man is a thinking reed; he is frail, but by the exercise of his mind he can know. Knowledge is an ennobling power that may lift him out of his otherwise muddied nature. But one finds no paeans to progress in the literature of Rebecca West; man has shown too much of his bestiality in the twentieth century for her to entertain the assumption that his religion or his science has helped him improve his fallible nature. The test Dame Rebecca has been most willing to use on any evidence she has examined is whether man's action leads to life or to death. If it leads to life it is to be cherished, if it leads to death it is to be shunned. In his nature man has the capacity for both; he should cultivate life, but often he does not. Rebecca West remains pessimistic.

Yet in our time Dame Rebecca must be counted among the grand old ladies of the feminist movement, thus affirming her belief that here progress was possible. Not many women alive today participated as she did in that great effort to secure women's suffrage. An even smaller group witnessed it from the vantage point she had. Yet today she is remembered more for her literature about other aspects of politics and history than she is for her feminist writing. The interests of the feminists today stress other concerns. They emphasize job opportunities, yet all three of the Fairfield sisters anticipated them by becoming distinguished professionals. Dame Rebecca showed great competence in her management of her professional life, so much so that we find her sitting on editorial boards and presiding over international literary associations. Contemporary feminists advocate alternative life-styles. In her way she had advocated as much, and she would approve those life-styles with one reservation, that they affirm the impulse toward life. Feminists today could learn from Rebecca West. We all can benefit from following her explorations of the feminine sensibility.

Dame Rebecca has attempted so many literary activities and has made such distinctive contributions to each of them that it seems inappropriate to state here that she should be remembered for any particular one of these contributions. Rather, after we have read her books, what does remain most vividly is a personality which brings to bear on any phenomenon it may encounter its active intensity. Above all else it wants to understand. It is responsive, discriminating in an inclusive sense, and emphatic. Most often its vision is darkly heroic, appropriate for the age it observed. Rebecca West has contributed a voice of sanity to a century in need of it.

Notes and References

Chapter One

1. Interview with Bernard Kalb, *Saturday Review of Literature,* March 19, 1955, p. 13.
2. George E. G. Catlin, ed., *The Rights of Women and The Subjection of Women* (London, 1929), verso of title page.
3. Margaret Fuller, "Woman in the Nineteenth Century" (1845), in *The Writings of Margaret Fuller* (New York, 1941), p. 125.
4. "The Nature of Woman. Every Home a Little Earlswood," *Clarion,* March 7, 1913, p. 6.
5. Clifton Fadiman, ed., *I Believe* (New York, 1939), p. 321.
6. "Mr. Chesterton in Hysterics. A Study in Prejudice," *Clarion,* November 14, 1913, p. 5.
7. "The Gospel According to Granville Barker," *Freewoman,* March 7, 1912, p. 307.
8. "The Sin of Self-Sacrifice," *Clarion,* December 12, 1913, p. 7.
9. "Much Worse Than Gaby Deslys. A Plea for Decency," *Clarion,* November 28, 1913, p. 9.
10. "Place of Women in Western Civilization—Excerpts of an Address before the Fabian Society in London," *New York Times,* December 16, 1928, section 10, p. 4.
11. "Woman Adrift," *Freewoman,* March 28, 1912, p. 368.
12. "A New Women's Movement. The Need for Riotous Living," *Clarion,* December 20, 1912, p. 3.
13. "The White Slave Traffic Bill. The Archbishop's Blood-Lust," *Clarion,* November 22, 1912, p. 4.
14. "The Bishop's Principles. Our Cause against the Church," *Clarion,* October 24, 1913, p. 7.
15. Ibid.
16. "Is a Woman's Place in the Home? A Debate between Rebecca West and Alfred Duff-Cooper," *New York Times,* September 20, 1925, section 9, p. 4.
17. "Mother or Capitalist. What the World Asks of Women," *Clarion,* September 19, 1913, p. 4.
18. "The Future of the Middle Classes: Women Who Are Parasites," *Clarion,* November 1, 1912, p. 3.
19. "The Life of Emily Davison," *Clarion,* June 20, 1913, p. 1.

20. In Britain the term *suffragist* was a respected, inclusive term for all women advocating the right to vote. The term *suffragette* was invented by the opponents of the women as a term of ridicule identifying the militant suffragists, particularly the members of the WSPU. However, these women quickly accepted the term as their distinctive identification.

21. "The Life of Emily Davison," p. 1.

22. Christabel Pankhurst's articles first appeared in the WSPU newsletter *Suffragette* and were published later in the book *Plain Facts about a Great Evil* (London, 1913).

23. "In Mentioning the Unmentionable. An Exhortation to Miss Pankhurst," *Clarion*, September 26, 1913, p. 5.

24. Ibid.

25. Ibid.

26. Ibid.

27. "Lynch Law. The Tragedy of Innocence," *Clarion*, October 17, 1913, p. 7.

28. Ibid.

29. "The Prig in Power. Whom God Hath Joined McKenna Puts Asunder," *Clarion*, January 10, 1913, p. 4.

30. Ibid.

31. Ibid.

32. "Socialists and Feminism. The Fate of the Limited Amendments," *Clarion*, January 24, 1913, p. 3.

33. Ibid.

34. "Mrs. Pankhurst," *The Post Victorians* (London, 1933), p. 479.

35. Ibid., p. 499.

36. Ibid., p. 500.

37. For much of the information on Rebecca West's life with H. G. Wells I am indebted to Gordon N. Ray, *H. G. Wells and Rebecca West* (New Haven, 1974).

Chapter Two

1. Frank Swinnerton, *The Georgian Scene* (New York, 1934), pp. 387–88.

2. Ethel Mannin, *Confessions and Impressions* (London, 1931), pp. 118–19.

3. Rupert Hart-Davis, *Hugh Walpole* (New York, 1952), p. 172.

4. Frank Swinnerton, *Figures in the Foreground* (London, 1963), p. 102.

5. *Ending in Earnest* (Garden City, N.Y., 1931), p. 31.

6. Ibid., p. 306.

7. "Mr. Yeats' Essays," *Daily News*, June 14, 1919, p. 2.

8. *The Strange Necessity* (London, 1928), p. 215.

9. "Extravagant Old Master," *Sunday Telegraph*, No. 249, November 7, 1965, p. 18.

10. *The Strange Necessity*, p. 200.

11. "Notes on Novels," *New Statesman*, May 13, 1922, p. 156.

12. Ibid., August 20, 1921, p. 548.

13. *The Strange Necessity*, p. 237.

14. Ibid., pp. 05-00.

15. Ibid., p. 65.

16. George Evelyn Hutchinson, "The Dome," *The Itinerant Ivory Tower* (New Haven, 1953).

17. *The Strange Necessity*, p. 95.

18. Ibid., p. 70.

19. *Henry James* (New York, 1916), p. 94.

20. Ibid., p. 61.

21. *The Strange Necessity*, p. 181.

22. "I Said to Me," *New York American*, October 13, 1931, no page number.

23. *Ending in Earnest*, p. 75.

24. "The Man from Main Street," *Nash's Pall Mall*, August 1935, p. 27.

25. *The Strange Necessity*, p. 271.

26. Ibid., p. 280.

27. *Arnold Bennett Himself* (New York, 1931), p 16

28. Ibid., p. 18.

29. *The Strange Necessity*, p. 200.

30. Ibid., p. 199.

31. *Ending in Earnest*, pp. 184-207.

32. Ibid., p. vii.

33. Ibid., pp. 304-305.

34. "The Benda Mask," *New York Herald Tribune Books*, December 29, 1929, p. 4.

35. *The Meaning of Treason* (London, 1956), p. 312.

36. Mr. Evelyn Waugh's Libel Action Settled," London *Times*, Dec. 14, 1956, p. 15; Evelyn Waugh, *The Diaries of Evelyn Waugh*. (Boston, 1976), p. 770.

37. *The Court and the Castle* (New Haven, 1957), pp. 238-39.

38. Ibid., p. 272.

Chapter Three

1. James D. Hart, *Oxford Companion to American Literature* (New York, 1965), p. 594.

2. "Duty of Harsh Criticism," *New Republic*, November 7, 1914, p. 19.

3. "Eroto-priggery," *New Republic*, March 13, 1915, p. 150.

4. *Lions and Lambs* (New York, 1928), p. 73.

5. Ibid., p. 112.

6. Ibid., p. 17.

7. Ibid., p. 21.

8. Ibid., p. 131.

9. "The New Deal. Part IV," *Time and Tide*, September 14, 1935, p. 1298.

10. H. G. Wells had set a precedent for her. He conceived his *Outline of History* during World War I. The stress of that war had sent him searching for answers just as the impending World War II impelled West's search. Both of them sought their answers in history.

11. "Books. On Making due Allowance for Distortion," *Time and Tide*, May 24, 1929, p. 623.

12. "Yogi and Commissar," *Time and Tide*, July 14, 1945, p. 576.

13. Ibid., p. 578.

14. "Notes on the Way," *Time and Tide*, May 5, 1934, p. 574.

15. "The Days of Long Hair and Fine Horses," *Time and Tide*, July 26, 1929, p. 906.

16. "My Father," *Sunday Telegraph*, December 30, 1962, p. 4.

17. *Black Lamb and Grey Falcon*, I, p. 1.

18. *St. Augustine*, p. 10.

19. *A Letter to a Grandfather* (London, 1933), p. 8.

20. Ibid., p. 10.

21. Ibid., p. 11.

22. Ibid., p. 35.

23. "Yogi and Commissar," *Time and Tide*, July 14, 1945, p. 576.

24. "War Aims," *Time and Tide*, November 28, 1939, p. 1466.

25. "Ashes in your Wine," *Time and Tide*, March 9, 1940, p. 252.

26. Ibid.

27. *A Letter to a Grandfather*, p. 44.

28. *Black Lamb and Grey Falcon*, I, p. 505.

29. Ibid., II, p. 481.

30. Ibid., I, p. 176.

31. Ibid., p. 523.

32. Ibid., II, p. 7.

33. Ibid., p. 536.

34. Ibid., p. 539.

35. Ibid., p. 294.

36. Ibid., II, p. 205.

37. Ibid., p. 403.

38. Ibid., p. 523.

Chapter Four

1. "The Meaning of Treason," *Harper's*, October 1947, p. 293.

2. Ibid.

3. Ibid.

4. Ibid., p. 290.

5. Ibid.

6. Ibid.

7. Ibid., p. 291.

8. Ibid., p. 290.

9. *The Meaning of Treason* (London, 1952), p. 280.

10. Ibid., p. 279.

11. Ibid., p. 281.

12. "Letter," *Time and Tide,* November 18, 1939, p. 1466.

13. C. P. Snow, *The New Men* (New York, 1954), pp. 220-21.

14. Ibid., p. 244.

15. Stow Persons, *The Decline of American Gentility* (New York, 1973), p. 32.

16. Margret Boveri, *Treason in the Twentieth Century* (New York, 1963), p. 348.

17. *The Meaning of Treason* (New York, 1947), p. 188.

18. Margret Boveri, *Treason in the Twentieth Century,* p. 40.

19. Ibid., p. 41.

20. *The Meaning of Treason* (New York, 1947), p. 191.

21. Ibid., p. 113.

22. Ibid.

23. Ibid.

24. Ibid., p. 207.

25. Ibid., p. 227.

26. *The Meaning of Treason* (London, 1952), p. 283.

27. Ibid., p. 308.

28. Ibid., p. 284.

29. *The Meaning of Treason* (London, 1956), p. 5.

30. Ibid., p. 6.

31. Ibid., p. 314.

32. *The New Meaning of Treason* (New York, 1964), p. 369.

33. Ibid.

34. *A Train of Powder* (New York, 1955), title page.

35. John Donne, *The Complete Poetry and Selected Prose of John Donne* (New York, 1952), p. 488.

36. *A Train of Powder,* p. 117.

37. Ibid., p. 247.

38. Ibid., pp. 249-50.

Chapter Five

1. Joseph Collins, *The Doctor Looks at Literature* (New York, 1923), p. 170.

2. *The Return of the Soldier* (New York, 1918), p. 46.

3. Patrick Braybrooke, *Novelists We Are Seven* (Freeport, N.Y., 1966), p. 143.

4. Peter Wolfe, *Rebecca West: Artist and Thinker* (Carbondale, Ill., 1971), p. 30.

5. *The Judge* (New York, 1922), p. 10.

6. Ibid., p. 51.

7. Ibid., p. 89.

8. Ibid., p. 90.

9. Ibid., p. 88.

10. Ibid., p. 120.

11. Ibid., pp. 258–59.

12. Gordon Ray, *H. G. Wells and Rebecca West*, p. 123.

13. *The Judge*, p. 490.

14. Frank Swinnerton, *The Georgian Scene*, p. 375.

15. Ray, *H. G. Wells . . .*, p. 185.

16. Sister Mary Margarita Orlich, *The Novels of Rebecca West: A Complex Unity* (Ann Arbor, 1967), p. 82.

17. *Lions and Lambs*, p. 131.

Chapter Six

1. *War Nurse* (New York, 1930), title page.

2. *Black Lamb and Grey Falcon*, II, p. 477.

3. *The Thinking Reed* (New York, 1938), verso to half-title.

4. Ibid., p. 331.

5. Ibid.

6. Ibid., p. 85.

7. Ibid., p. 131.

8. Ibid., p. 345.

9. Ibid., p. 346.

10. Ibid., p. 89.

11. *The Fountain Overflows* (New York, 1956), p. 218.

12. Ibid., p. 307.

13. The theme of clairvoyance in *The Fountain Overflows* reflects West's personal interest intensified by her conviction that she had experienced moments of clairvoyance during World War II.

14. "I Regard Marriage with Fear and Horror," *Hearst's International-Cosmopolitan*, November 1925, p. 66.

15. Ibid.

16. Ibid.

17. "My Father," *Sunday Telegraph*, No. 100, December 30, 1962, p. 4.

18. Ibid., p. 4.

19. "I Regard Marriage with Fear and Horror," p. 67.

20. *The Fountain Overflows*, p. 167.

21. Ibid., p. 313.

22. *The Birds Fall Down* (New York, 1966), p. 308.

23. Ibid., p. 269.

24. Ibid., p. 181.

25. Rebecca West is presently at work on the second book in the trilogy, entitled *The Real Night.* A section from this novel is included in *Rebecca West. A Celebration* (New York, 1977).

Selected Bibliography

PRIMARY SOURCES

Arnold Bennett Himself. New York: John Day Co., 1931.
The Birds Fall Down. New York: Viking Press, 1966.
Black Lamb and Grey Falcon. London: Macmillan & Co., 1941.
The Court and the Castle. New Haven: Yale University Press, 1957.
D. H. Lawrence. London: Martin Secker, 1930.
Ending in Earnest. Freeport, N.Y.: Books for Libraries Press, 1967.
The Fountain Overflows. New York: Viking Press, 1956.
Harriet Hume. Garden City, N.Y.: Doubleday, Doran & Co., 1930.
The Harsh Voice. Garden City, N.Y.: Doubleday, Doran & Co., 1937.
Henry James. New York: Henry Holt & Co., 1916.
The Judge. New York: George H. Doran Co., 1922.
A Letter to a Grandfather. London: Hogarth Press, 1933.
Lions and Lambs. With David Low. New York: Harcourt, Brace & Co., 1928.
The Meaning of Treason. New York: Viking Press, 1947.
The Meaning of Treason. London: Macmillan, 1949.
The Meaning of Treason. London: Reprint Society, 1952.
The Meaning of Treason. London: Pan Books Ltd., 1956.
"Mrs. Pankhurst," in *The Post Victorians.* Introduction by W. R. Inge. London: Nicholson & Watson, 1933.
The Modern "Rake's Progress." With David Low. London: Hutchinson, 1934.
The New Meaning of Treason. New York: Viking Press, 1964.
"Notes on Novels," in *New Statesman,* April 17, 1920 to December 2, 1922.
The Return of the Soldier. New York: Century Co., 1918.
"Reviews," in *New York Herald Tribune,* Book Section. October 10, 1926, to February 7, 1932.
St. Augustine. New York: D. Appleton & Co., 1933.
The Strange Necessity. London: Jonathan Cape, 1928.
The Thinking Reed. New York: Viking Press, 1938.
"This I Believe," in *I Believe.* Clifton Fadiman, Ed. London: Allen and Unwin, 1940.
A Train of Powder. New York: Viking Press, 1955.
The Vassall Affair. London: Sunday Telegraph, no date.

Weekly columns in the *Clarion*. London: September 27, 1912, to December 12, 1913.

SECONDARY SOURCES

1. Bibliography
HUTCHINSON, G. EVELYN. *A Preliminary List of the Writings of Rebecca West*. New Haven: Yale University Library, 1957. This bibliography is an invaluable help to anyone interested in Rebecca West's critical and political writings. The bibliography includes most of her writing between 1912 and 1951. It has been announced that Professor Hutchinson is collecting material for an updated edition.

2. Other Books
BARTH, ALAN. *The Loyalty of Free Men*. New York: Archon, 1965. A well-argued defense of personal freedoms guaranteed in the Bill of Rights within the context of the threats to them that developed in the McCarthy era.

BOVERI, MARGRET. *Treason in the Twentieth Century*. New York: G. P. Putnam's Sons, 1963. A wide ranging, thoughtful study of treason during the political turmoil in Europe during World War II. It explores aspects of treason that West's study does not.

CATLIN, GEORGE E. G., ed. *The Rights of Women and The Subjection of Women*. London: J. M. Dent & Sons., 1929. These two essays are the primary arguments for women's rights in nineteenth-century Britain.

FULLER, MARGARET *The Writings of Margaret Fuller*. New York: Viking Press, 1941. Margaret Fuller occupies the same position in the feminist movement in the United States that Mary Wollstonecraft does in Britain.

HUTCHINSON, GEORGE EVELYN. "The Dome," in *The Itinerant Ivory Tower*. New Haven: Yale University Press, 1953. This essay explores the philosophical implications of Rebecca West's work.

HYNES, SAMUEL. "Introduction" to *Rebecca West: A Celebration*. New York: Viking, 1977. This essay was written originally as a review of Peter Wolfe's critical study of Rebecca West's writing. The essay presents an historical and critical overview of her work. It stresses the difficulty of identifying her with any school or movement.

ORLICH, SISTER MARY MARGARITA. *The Novels of Rebecca West: A Complex Unity*. Ann Arbor: University Microfilms, 1967. This study was prepared as a doctoral dissertation. It presents a generally commendatory estimate of West's novels. It stresses the moral characteristics of the novels.

RAY, GORDON N. *H. G. Wells and Rebecca West*. New Haven: Yale

University Press, 1974. Aside from short passages in biographies of H. G. Wells, this book is the first attempt to present the biographical details of a part of Rebecca West's life. It is based on the letters H. G. Wells sent to Rebecca West and on her recollections of their relationship. In preparing it, Gordon Ray worked closely with Rebecca West.

SWINNERTON, FRANK. *The Georgian Scene*. New York: Farrar and Rinehart, 1934. This is a fine literary history of the period written by one who knew many of the people he presents.

TINDALL, WILLIAM YORK. *Forces in Modern British Literature: 1885–1956*. New York: Random House, 1956. Tindall's book is useful in its categorization of the writers of this transitional period. For a study of Rebecca West, it is useful for its presentation of background material.

WOLFE, PETER. *Rebecca West: Artist and Thinker*. Carbondale: Southern Illinois University Press, 1971. This book was prepared for Crosscurrents, a series of modern critical studies. It traces certain of West's themes through her works. The author depends primarily on her books, thus leaving out important aspects of her work. He praises her primarily for her nonfiction.

WOLFER, VERENA ELSBETH. *Rebecca West: Kunsttheorie und Romanschaffen*. Bern: Francke Verlag, 1972. This book also was prepared as a dissertation. It attempts to establish relations between West's creative and critical works.

Index

181

RITTER LIBRARY
BALDWIN-WALLACE COLLEGE